FOLLOWING A SINGLE SCHOOL AND RULES FOR ISSUING *FATWĀS*

Imran Ahsan Khan Nyazee

Center for Excellence in Research
Islamabad

Center for Excellence in Research,
Head Office: No. 103, Street 2, PTV Colony,
Shahpur, Islamabad,
Pakistan 44000

First Published: 2016

CENTER FOR EXCELLENCE IN RESEARCH

TABLE OF CONTENTS

Ch. 1 Introduction 5

Ch. 2 The Meaning of "School of Law" and Following a Single *Madhhab* 11

2.1 The Views of Modern Scholars on Why a Particular School Should be Followed 11

2.2 The *Uṣūlī* Argument for Following a Single School 18

2.2.1 The Nature of the *Qawā'id Uṣūliyyah*: the Basis of the Schools of Law 18

2.2.2 A School of Law Then is a Unique Body of Rules of Interpretation 19

2.2.3 The Analogy of Portability and Staying Within the School 20

Ch. 3 *Taqlīd* and its Implementation Within the School 23

3.1 The Meaning and Implications of *Taqlīd* . . . 24

3.1.1 The Literal Meaning of *Taqlīd* 24

3.1.2 The Technical Meanings of *Taqlīd* 24

3.1.3 *Taqlīd* in the Pakistani Legal System . . . 27

3.2 The Primary Function of a School of Law . . . 27

3.3 The Resources of the School: Jurists, Issues and Texts 29

3.3.1 The Hierarchy of Jurists Within a School . 29

3.3.2 The Hierarchy of Issues Within a School . 32

3.3.3 The Hierarchy of Texts Within a School . 33

3.4 The Integral Bond Between the Four Sunni Schools 41

Ch. 4 **Separating the *Mujtahids* from the Non-*Mujtahids*** **49**
4.1 The Necessity of a School 49
4.2 Preserving the School System 52
4.2.1 Understanding the Hierarchy of Jurists Within a School 54
4.2.2 Understanding the Hierarchy of the Earlier Rulings 56
4.2.3 Understanding the Hierarchy of Texts Within the School 56
4.2.4 The Result of the Three Steps 57

Ch. 5 **What is a *Fatwā* and Who is a *Muftī*?** **59**
5.1 What is a *Fatwā*? 59
5.2 Who is a *Muftī*? 61
5.3 Recalling the Meaning of *Ijtihād* and *Taqlīd* . . 64

Ch. 6 **The *Mujtahids* Within the School and Following the *Qawl* (Opinion) of the Imām, Always** **69**
6.1 Identifying the Issue 69
6.2 The Activity of the *Mujtahids* Within the School 70
6.3 Is it Mandatory for the *Muqallid Muftī* to Follow the View of the Imam and no One Else? . 72
6.4 In What Cases is the *Qawl* (Opinion) of the Imām or of the School to be Given Up? 78
6.4.1 "If a *Ḥadīth* is Proved Sound, Adopt it as my View"—Abū Ḥanīfah 78
6.4.1.1 Can the Tradition be Adopted? . . 79
6.4.1.2 If the Tradition is Adopted, the Jurist Must Stay Within His School 81
6.4.1.3 The Vital Role of Traditions and Modern Issues 82
6.4.2 Picking and Choosing or the Varieties of *Talfīq* 84
6.4.2.1 The Meaning in General 84
6.4.2.2 Using the Qāḍī as the Standard . . 85

6.4.2.3 Rules That Prohibit Picking and Choosing 89
6.4.3 Giving up the View of the School on the Basis of 'Urf and the Changes Over Time . 95
6.4.3.1 The Nature of the Change Expected 95
6.4.3.2 The Meaning of *'Urf* as the Basis of Change 96
6.4.3.3 Bringing Order Into the *'Urf* Methodology 98

Ch. 7 Important Rules in *Sharḥ 'Uqud Rasm al-Muftī* 101
7.1 Basic Rules for the *Muftī* 102
7.2 Who are the Mashā'ikh 104
7.3 Additional Rules 105

Ch. 8 What Needs to be Done 107
8.1 Training for Dealing With Variation in Facts . 107
8.2 Methodology for Areas Not Covered by the School 109

Bibliography 111

Appendices 113

A Ḥanafī Sources: *Uṣūl al-Fiqh* 115

B Ḥanafī Sources: *Fiqh* 123

Index 141

CHAPTER 1

INTRODUCTION

فَمَالِ هٰؤُلَآءِ الْقَوْمِ لَا يَكَادُونَ يَفْقَهُونَ حَدِيثًا

What hath come to these people that they fail to understand a simple statement (Qur'ān 4 : 78)

Al-Ḥaskafī says in the beginning of his book that no one, other than the Prophets, knows what Allah desires for them. The exception, he says, are the jurists, for it is about them that Allah has said: "He for whom Allah wills his blessings is granted the *fiqh* of Dīn."[1] He thus indicates the high status of the discipline of *fiqh* and the consequent blessings for the person who pursues this knowledge. Indeed, the issuing of *fatwās* is the noblest of all human activities, but at the same time it is the most perilous of duties. The task of the *muftī* is almost similar to that of the *qāḍī* or even more extensive, because the *muftī* gives rulings in cases of dispute and also guides the subject in personal matters pertaining to this world or the next. The judgment of the *qāḍī* is binding, while the *fatwā* of the *muftī* is not binding. Nevertheless, the responsibility is immense and the task colossal. In this module, we will address the complexities and difficulties that beset the pursuit of this noble profession.

We have covered a lot of ground in the previous modules. Anyone who has gone through all the texts is by now fully aware of how the system works in traditional Islamic law and what additional requirements are imposed by the needs of the modern world. In any legal system, the ultimate test is how legal problems are solved with justice and how rights are secured. This is

1. We will be referring to al-Ḥaskafī as the *matn* of Ibn 'Ābidīn's work, for ease of reference, although the work has been published separately as well. Muḥammad Amīn Ibn 'Ābidīn, *Radd al-Muḥtār 'alā al-Durr al-Mukhtār Sharḥ Tanwīr al-Abṣār*, 12 vols. (Riyadh: Dār 'Ālam al-Kutub, 2003), vol. 1, 138.

reflected in the quality of the decisions rendered. Islamic law, being a religious law, operates at two levels: the issuance of *fatwas* and the rendering of decisions. *Fatwas* may be compared with legal opinions in another legal system. *The word used in Roman law for fatwā was "responsa."* The difference is that *fatwas* are related to the moral as well as the legal domain. In other words, the ordinary Muslim may sometimes ignore what the state law is and follow the *fatwā*.

Today, we often witness this in the case of family law in a country like Pakistan. For example, the law considers every divorce, irrespective of the number of times it is pronounced, as a single repudiation and assigns consequences accordingly.[2] The affected individual, on the other hand, takes three repudiations into account, if three have actually been pronounced, because he considers himself morally bound by traditional Islamic law; he ignores the state law. In addition to this, state law has radically altered the rule about *khul'*, converting it from an out of court settlement between the parties—which the *qāḍī* merely confirms—to a mandatory form of divorce that is available to a woman who just has to file an application seeking *khul'*. As this goes against the established law of the school, there might be people who will not accept it morally or on the basis of traditional Islamic law, and remarriage of such a divorced woman may be considered an unlawful act. Others might argue that a ruling issued by a judge removes all disagreements about an issue, but this argument is not acceptable to the former—who considers it morally unsound—as a *muqallid* judge cannot go against the established rules of the school.

Beyond this, the ordinary Muslim seeks *fatwas* for everyday matters and this has been going on for more than a thousand years. As a result, the institution of seeking *fatwas* has become extremely important and the system of issuing *fatwas* exceedingly complex. The modern world has brought a host of new problems with it and this has added to the complexity and has heightened the activity. The seeking of *fatwas* has, therefore, spilled over to the Internet and there are many institutions trying to meet this

2. See, Muslim Family Laws Ordinance, 1961.

need.

A very important point that emerges from the study of the previous modules is that the Ḥanafī school, or any other school for that matter, is a "system" for deriving rules from the texts and implementing them for regulating the lives of the subjects. Within this school, the Imām A'ẓam and and his immediate disciples enjoy immense respect and a lofty status. Nevertheless, the school is a "system" that has taken centuries to build and refine through the contribution of hundreds of jurists in the early centuries. All these jurists have respected positions in the system. Anyone who fails to realize the significance of the system, as distinct from the jurists, is likely to fall into confusion at some stage or at some point. In some ways, this entire course has been directed towards the indication of this significance. Understanding the school as a system has a huge impact on the debates surrounding the meaning of *muftī*, his sources and qualifications. Consequently, the reader should keep this fact in view when trying to understand the underlying issues.

In this module, we move from the theoretical framework of interpretation in Islamic law to the applied field of issuing *fatwas* and rendering judgments. We will try to unravel the underlying issues in the light of the debates among the jurists of the Ḥanafī school as to what is the best method of issuing *fatwās*. It may be stated at the outset, however, that the field of *fatwās* is not easy to understand, especially due to the existence of the complexity indicated, and due to the different views of the jurists that are often read out of context and become a source of confusion. The jurists assume that the context is obvious, but for the reader this is not always true, just as it has not been true for some later jurists. To undertand this topic, some of the material discussed in the previous modules will often be recalled to elaborate the situation.

Another important point to understand is that a school of law does not come into being all at once, as if by magic. It is a lengthy process that often spans centuries. The foundations laid in the initial stages give rise to huge bodies of principles, presumptions and rules. These principles, presumptions and rules are gradually refined through a variety of views generated by the jurists. Over time, the propositions of the school begin to crystallize and mature. This raises the need for stability within the school as a perpetually fluid situation cannot be allowed to continue if the school has to survive and its original foundations have to be preserved. This is exactly what happened in the Ḥanafī school and also in other schools. As the centuries passed more and more restrictions were placed on the liberty of jurists within the school for the sake of the system; this is done in every legal system. The earlier freedom enjoyed by the jurists slowly came to be controlled through rules that are collectively referred to as *taqlīd*. The doctrine of *taqlīd* was essential, because giving absolute freedom to the jurist to deal with the law as they liked would have meant disruption within the school and its doctrines and even the uprooting of the very foundations on which the school had been so carefully erected.[3]

The laws derived by the jurists from the texts of the Qur'ān and the *Sunnah* were able to deal with most of the problems faced by societies up to medieval times. These were laws that were not likely to change much over time as they had direct links to the texts of the Qur'ān and the *Sunnah*, which could not be altered. Certain parts of the law that were necessary for the administration of the state, were left to the rulers. The jurists provided broad guidelines and methodologies for keeping such changeable laws within the norms of the *sharī'ah*, but did not provide the details as these laws were alterable anyway. The rulers sometimes conformed to these guidelines and at other times they did not, but there was a constant pressure that all such provisions conform to the dictates of the *sharī'ah*.[4] It is the same pressure that we find today in many Muslim majority countries for the Islamization of the laws. Consequently, many new laws, institutions and even a parallel system of courts were designed. In short, legal problems faced by Muslims up to the period of colonization were always solved by these systems one way or the other. Colonization altered these systems

3. For a complete explanation of the doctrine of *taqlīd*, see Imran Ahsan Khan Nyazee, *Islamic Jurisprudence* (Islamabad: Federal Law House, 2013), 375.
4. Imran Ahsan Khan Nyazee, *Theories of Islamic Law: The Methodology of Ijtihād* (Islamabad: Federal Law House, 2007), See the chapter of the doctrines of *ḥadd*.

radically and made them defunct or removed them from the scene altogether.

Advances in science and technology in the last few centuries, on a scale unprecedented in human history, brought radical changes to the world. Wars on a global scale brought in many new international arrangements. Colonization gave way to greater international interaction among nations as well as global commerce, which in turn gave rise to revolutionary changes in the nature of commerce and banking. It was only after these changes had set in, and with a gap of several centuries, that Islamic law reemerged on the scene in the Muslim world. Muslim scholars had been working during this period, but had focused mainly on the part of the law that was directly linked to the texts. The institutions, rules and courts that the earlier Muslim rulers had erected had disappeared from the scene. Yet, the restrictions placed on the jurists through the doctrine of *taqlīd* were still in place. Many started seeing these restrictions as a hindrance for the development of Islamic law and its reform, rather than as an essential doctrine that had brought stability to the system and preserved it over the ages. Attempts were also made to come up with solutions within these restrictions. A movement was seen from one school to several in search of new solutions. Unique ways of creating new opinions were devised including patching up opinions to form new ones. These efforts have not been enough to resolve new issues and problems. Under the weight of the restrictions many jurists have succumbed to *sharī'ah* solutions provided by economists and other experts, who have no expertise in Islamic law. This has been noticeable in the area of banking and commerce. In the meantime, modern problems cry out for valid *sharī'ah* solutions. A huge and gaping void exists. If this void is not filled by solutions coming from the depths of Islamic law, there is a danger of this law becoming irrelevant for the modern world; signs of which have already become visible.

In this module we will first deal with the a major question that is asked by many and for which no scientific or technical arguments have been provided as yet. The strongest argument given simply appeals to the piety of the earlier Imāms and the fact that they deserve to be followed. The assertion is undeniable, but arguments must arise from within the system to justify the following of a single school. Related to this is the meaning of *taqlīd,* which we have explained elsewhere but would like to recall in brief along with the function of the school. Having done this, we will try to assess the system of *taqlīd* that has been described for us. This assessment will then be followed by the description of the meaning, nature and method of *fatwās*. There are many points that are debated by the jurists and we will try to understand the implications of these debates. The important issues of following another school, choosing opinions and *talfīq* will also be taken up. Once we have done all this, our goal will be to lay down certain best practices for the writing and issuing of *fatwās*, especially on new issues.

CHAPTER 2

THE MEANING OF "SCHOOL OF LAW" AND FOLLOWING A SINGLE *MADHHAB*

Many people have started questioning the basis for following a single school in matters of the *sharī'ah.* A number of reasons are advanced for not following a school, but the real aim appears to be to eliminate the authority of the jurists over the masses. Once eliminated, this authority is to be replaced by some kind of natural law or Neo-Mu'tazilah form of reasoning. From the other side, many reasons are advanced for following a single school, but many of these arguments can be easily refuted. In this chapter, we will try to advance a technical reason as the true basis for following a single school.

2.1 The Views of Modern Scholars on Why a Particular School Should be Followed

Following a single school of Islamic law is the first restriction that is faced not only by the jurist, but also by the layman. Resistance to this restriction is becoming stronger by the day, so much so that some have even questioned whether the following of schools is a *bid'ah* (innovation). Consequently, many scholars have tried to elaborate why it is necessary to follow a single school. The learned Muftī Taqi Usmani wrote a very comprehensive document on the issue. This has now been translated into English.[5] We will rely on this document alone as the learned Taqi Usmani has, as usual, dealt with the topic in a very comprehensive manner, and most other scholars offer the same arguments. We will attempt to organize the arguments given by the learned scholar through ex-

5. *Legal Status of Following a Madhhab.* It is available on the Internet at `www.kalamullah.com/Books/LegalStatusOfFollowingAMadhab.pdf`.

cerpts from this text. No attempt will be made to correct or edit the words, except obvious errors. The learned scholar presents the following arguments:

- **Islamic law is complex and requires specialists. The jurists are these specialists:** The issues of Islamic law are very complex and such complexity requires specialization. The jurists are the specialists who deal with Islamic law. "So ask the people of remembrance if you know not."[6] This verse implies that the specialist be followed. A verse says: "O you who believe! Follow Allah; follow the Messenger and those of authority (Amr) amongst you."[7] A large number of authorities are quoted in the document to show that the term "those in authority" means the jurists. The words of the Qur'ān, "And if you dispute, then refer it to Allah and the Messenger if you really do believe in Allah and in the Last Day,"[8] are not directed at the layman. The verse is interpreted to mean that it is a command for the jurists.

- **The jurists were pious persons and such persons should be followed:** This meaning has also been derived from the the Qur'ān where it means following prophets and good people in religious affairs: "They are the ones whom We guided, so follow their guidance."[9] Follow the good and pious people, for some of them may really be the guided ones.

- ***Taqlīd* or following the opinion of another was prevalent even in the time of the Companions (R), but later a need was felt for systematization:** *Taqlīd*, which means following someone else's opinion was to be found even in the time of the Companions (R), but a few generations later a dire need was felt for systematization. Opinion without knowledge was discouraged. It was the responsibility of a person who was not a scholar to ask someone who had knowledge of

6. Qur'ān 16:90.
7. Qur'ān 4:59.
8. Qur'ān 4:59
9. Qur'ān 6:90.

the Qur'ān and Sunnah. If the knowledgeable person gave an erroneous *fatwā*, the burden of sin is on the *muftī* and not on the questioner. Certain historical changes occurred and these led to a need for systemization.

- **Ultimately, the jurists saw a need for drawing the boundaries of *taqlīd* and of the following of one school:** The scholars saw that there was a need to demarcate the practice of *taqlīd*. For reasons of administration and to avoid the possibility of contradictions amongst the scholars of differing *ijtihād* over a primary source, people were encouraged to follow only one Imam and *mujtahid* instead of referring to several. This idea gained hegemony during the third and fourth century Hijrah. Hence, it has been the dictum of the vast majority of the *Ummah* for subsequent centuries, and scholars themselves have conformed to *taqlīd* of a particular Imam. The jurists were concerned at the decay of piety and devoutness amongst the Muslim populous, devoutness being the norm during the time of the Companions (R). They feared that the scruples of subsequent generations would not be as elevated as those of the first three generations (Salaf). If under these circumstances, the door of following an Imam in general were unconditional, inadvertently desires would become the commanding principle. A person left freely to adopt the view which suited him best and abandon the *fatwā* which did not meet his "standards" of comfort begs the question upon what basis is the "non-scholar" to choose between two contrary *fatwās* if not one's own *nafs* (desires). It is clear that this line of action would result in people using Islamic law as a triviality to entertain the lower self. No Muslim scholar of any repute has validated this kind of practice.

- **Becoming a *mujtahid* was no longer possible:** The *taqlīd* of four Imams became popular throughout Muslim cities and the *taqlīd* of other scholars was forsaken. The doors of diverse opinions were closed because so many academic terms were being used to denote so many different concepts and because it had become so difficult to reach the stage of a *mujtahid*. There was the apprehension that the title of *mujtahid* might be attributed to one who was not worthy, or someone who was inauthentic (and could not be trusted) in his opinion and in his religious practice. Scholars declared that attaining the stage of a *mujtahid* was not possible and restricted people to follow a particular Imam. They prevented people from following Imams alternately as this was tantamount to playing [with Islam]. This discussion is based on the statement of Ibn Khaldūn, *Muqaddimah* (Egypt: Makatab Tijariyah Kubrah, n.d.), 448.

- **Following a school is not *bid'ah* (innovation):** A question might arise from this analysis: How can something that was not necessary during the times of the Companions and their followers become necessary for people who came after them? An eloquent reply has been offered by Shah Waliyullah:

  > It is mandatory that there should be someone in the community (*Ummah*) who knows details of particular rules and laws with their reasoning and proofs. The people of truth have unanimously agreed to this premise. A science or action which is necessary to fulfill a mandatory action also becomes mandatory in itself. For example, the predecessors did not write the sayings of the Prophet (sallalahu alaihi wa sallam). Today writing and documenting Hadith has become necessary, because the only way we can know and learn Hadith is by knowing the books of Hadith. Likewise, the predecessors did not engage in studying syntax and etymology, because their language was Arabic, and advanced study of these ancillary sciences was not required. Today, learning these sciences has become mandatory since the language has drifted considerably from the original language of Arabic. Based on this account, one

> must draw an analogy for proving that following one particular Imam and Mujtahid is sometimes necessary and sometimes not necessary. [*Al-Inṣāf fī Bayān Sabab Ikhtilāf*: 57/59. Published by Matba' Mujtabai, 1935. Ibid 69/71.]

Shah Waliyyullah hinted toward the chaos and corruption which was prevented by restricting *taqlīd* to one Mujtahid: "In short, following the Mujtahids was a subtle inspiration which Allah unveiled to the scholars. A consensus arose among the rightly guided scholars, to its indispensability. Knowingly or unknowingly, it was upon this inspiration that the vast majority of the ummah united." He wrote in another place: "The Ummah has unanimously agreed upon the validity of following one of the four schools of thought—which have been organized and documented. There are many obvious benefits in this, especially today when determination has dwindled; when desires have penetrated our consciousness and gloating in one's own opinion is seen as a virtue."

- **Why only four schools?** This begs the question: if following one particular Mujtahid is indispensable, why the need to restrict *taqlīd* to only the four schools of thought? Several great Imams and Mujtahids have occupied the pages of Islamic scholastic history such personages as Sufyān Thawri, Imam Awzā'ī, Abdullah ibn Mubarak, Ishaq ibn Rahwayh, Imam Bukhari, Ibn Abi Layla, Ibn Sibrimah, Hasan ibn Salih and many others. Are all Mujtahids not equally qualified to be followed? Such a contention is valid in principle, but it is not effectively possible. The schools of thought of the Mujtahids mentioned above are not systematically documented. Had their schools been formally codified and structured similar to the major four schools, then there would be no hindrance to following them. Unfortunately, their schools do not exist formally, nor have the original sources of the schools survived. To follow such schools would therefore prove difficult.

- **Why one particular school and why not all?** Shah Waliyyullah, has allocated a whole chapter to this discussion in his book: "Iqdul Jeed" and called it: "The Chapter of Emphasising following one of these four schools of thought and denouncing the idea of forsaking them." He started the chapter by saying: "You should know that following these four schools have tremendous public advantages and benefits. Forsaking them is wrought with mischief and harms. We will explain this with many inferences ...."

  Mawlana Taqi Usmani says: He then goes on to explain the many reasons which I will paraphrase in points instead of translating a very lengthy passage. It is incumbent to rely upon the early predecessors if one is to understand Islamic law. The only way for us to do this is either to determine that the statements of the predecessors have been transmitted to us via sound chain of narrators or to read their statements, which are documented in reliable books. It is necessary to establish that these statements have actually been trusted and used by other scholars. Finally, if their statements are open to several meanings, then the most preferred meaning be adopted. Occasionally, the statement of a certain Mujtahid may appear to be general but in fact it may be quite specific, which would be recognised by the scholars who have studied his school of thought. Thus, it is necessary that the statements of this certain Mujtahid be documented, understood and explained such that the rationale is emphasised. If a certain Mujtahid has not had his statements codified then such a Madhhab should not be relied upon. In our age, the four prominent schools of thought share this advantage whereas other schools do not.

  Finally, if giving a Fatwa based on any of the earlier scholars and their schools of thought were to be made permissible, then corrupt scholars would take advantage of the Shari'ah and base their Fatwas on the statements of any of the predecessors. This would inevitably open the door to the abuse of their statements. Corrupt scholars would be asked to justify selfish desires by quoting pious predecessors. Relying upon following the vast majority of the community would arrest the drift to chaos within the Shari'ah.

The above arguments are good and the efforts of the learned Mufti Taqi Usmani have to be appreciated. We can raise some questions, but that will lengthen the description unnecessarily. The only point we will raise is that some people today may not find some of the arguments to be very convincing. For example, they may say that every legal system is complex and is in need of specialists, but that does not mean we should adopt a single theory of law as a valid theory; legal systems continue to work without doing so. Again, there are many pious scholars today who can be followed. Today, we have the means of checking the acts of corrupt scholars who plagiarize the work of other schools and present it as their own. The work of scholars who do not belong to the four accepted schools also stands documented. The general populace, with the spread of education, is quite capable of determining the chains of narrations from the published material. There may be benefits in not following a single school as it will provide freedom to deal with the multitude of problems faced by the Ummah today. Consequently, scholars can get together and decide that it is no longer necessary to follow a single school.[10]

In short, even a simple response may be enough to show that the very good arguments provided may not be sufficient to convince everyone. In reality, this is exactly what has happened and many educated people are approaching the *aḥadīth* on their own and concluding what the law must be on a particular point. The situation is rapidly becoming what may be called a "free for all." It is indeed a dangerous development for Islamic law.

True arguments must be discovered and for doing so we have to turn to *uṣūl al-fiqh* again.

10. In fact, the Neo-Mu'tazilah in the West are trying to do exactly this.

2.2 The *Uṣūlī* Argument for Following a Single School

The true argument for following a single school, and also for not floating between schools, is to be found in the Discipline of *Uṣūl al-Fiqh* itself. In all the previous modules we have indicated that understanding the meaning of *'ilm uṣūl al-fiqh* is essential for many things.[11] It is now time for the reader to test his understanding of the meaning.

2.2.1 The Nature of the *Qawā'id Uṣūliyyah*: the Basis of the Schools of Law

For the Uṣūlī, the term *uṣūl* implies "a body of principles" that he uses to interpret the texts, as has been elaborated right from module I. As these *uṣūl* or rules contain within them the meaning of the "sources of Islamic law", the *uṣūlī* does not emphasise the meaning of *uṣūl* as sources, rather he focuses on the rules, which are the rules of interpretation. He hands over these rules to the jurists of the school (the *fuqahā'*), who use them to create the knowledge base of the law also called *fiqh*. It is better to call these *uṣūl* principles for reasons that should be obvious to the reader by now.

We have tried, in the previous modules, to list as many of these rules of interpretation as was possible in documents of this nature. In addition to the rules of interpretation,[12] we have also listed many of the presumptions that are used for the interpretation of facts and for other purposes.[13] There is no need to repeat those rules here and the reader can very quickly review the rules by looking at the frames in which these rules were written.

11. This has been explained in detail in the first module on the secrets of *uṣūl*. For a simpler explantation, please see Nyazee, *Islamic Jurisprudence*.
12. Most of these rules are listed in module II.
13. See module III.

2.2.2 A School of Law Then is a Unique Body of Rules of Interpretation

We have seen in the previous modules that some *qawānīn* are accepted unanimously by all schools, while others are not. The total body of such rules accepted by one school differs to some extent from the set adopted by another school. This is what makes them distinct schools of law. Within a school, the *uṣūl* adopted are analytically consistent, that is, they do not clash with each other, rather they complement one another, like flowers in a bouquet. Across school boundaries there may be a clash among such *uṣūl*, with the colours showing incompatibility.

Theoretically, the body of such rules is adopted by the founder of a school. Thus, for the Ḥanafī school, the rules were adopted by Abū Ḥanīfah and those for the Malikī school by Imām Mālik. It is true that all the detailed rules may not have been laid down by the founder, but he did establish a base on which the details were constructed. In fact, we sometimes find the immediate disciples of the Imam trying to argue about these *qawānīn* as well, but this is rare and it was done only in the earlier formative stages of the school.

The body of rules adopted by each school amounts to the theory of interpretation or theory of law of that school.[14] Each theory of law is somewhat different from that of another school and has an impact on the *aḥkām* derived. Understanding the nature of the *uṣūl* by relating them to each school is extremely important for understanding the discipline of *uṣūl al-fiqh*. It is also for this reason that picking and choosing opinions randomly across school boundaries is looked down upon and deemed inappropriate. We shall have more to say about this in the section of portability below.

---

14. For an explanation about the meaning of theories in Islamic law, see Nyazee, *Theories of Islamic Law*,

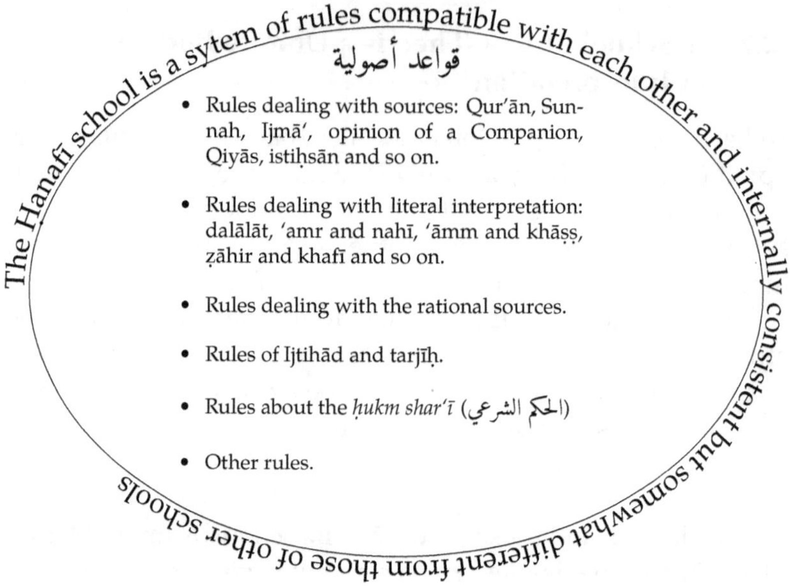

Imagine each school as a vase; four identical vases. The base is the same, but the flowers arranged in them have different colours. The jurists of one school prefer one set of colours, while those of the other schools prefer other sets. There is another integral bond between the Sunni schools beyond this too, and we have explained that later.

2.2.3 The Analogy of Portability and Staying Within the School

The distinctions mentioned above should have made matters clear about the necessity of following a school of law. We will, however, go ahead and use an analogy from the computer world as most people use computers today and will find the explanations easier. It may not be a perfect analogy, but it will help.

There are different operating systems in which people work today: Windows, Unix (Linux), Macintosh OS and so on. Now there are certain files that can easily be read across all systems due to their portability. These may be like the PDF (portable document format), postscript files, image files and so on. Beyond this, a program file or even another file of one system may not open or work in another operating system. Thus, the Microsoft Office or Word program made for windows will not work on the Macintosh or even in Unix. This was from the perspective of software. Hardware, too, explains our analogy if we say that each microchip (Motorolla or other) has its own instruction set that differs from the instruction set of other chips. The position in the schools of Islamic law is quite similar.

A person working in the Ḥanafī school should, therefore, remain in the Ḥanafī school. Choosing things from one school and pasting them into the other school will not work. Thus, taking an opinion based on *istiḥsān* and pasting it into the Shāfi'ī school will not work, because that school considers *istiḥsān* to be a nullity. Likewise, an opinion based on the rule that the opinion of a Companion is binding may not work in the Shāfi'ī school, which considers such an opinion not to be binding. Go on to other points of difference and you will start realizing the significance of this statement. For example, the system of literal construction or *dalālāt* used by the Ḥanafīs is radically different from that followed by other schools.

A person may say: what is the difference, when we follow one opinion we are following one acceptable school and when we follow another we are following another acceptable school? This question is excusable if it comes from a layman, but in the case of a jurist it is unpardonable. If the jurist, who knows the systems, says this, he will be saying in one statement: *istiḥsān* is valid and not valid; opinion of a Companion is binding and non-binding; the general word is *qaṭ'ī* and *zannī*. This amounts to playing with the law, which is a sacred law. For the same reason, floating between schools is not pardonable.

If the layman, or a jurist for that matter, likes some opinions in the other school, he should move completely to the other school. Staying in one school and choosing pleasing opinions from other schools is not appropriate.

The learned Abu Zahrā, at the end of his book on *uṣūl*, attempts to lay down certain conditions for picking and choosing from different schools, or as some say floating between schools. The conditions reduced to the basics appear to say that the jurist must be a good man, he should do so honestly and not while pursuing his whims (*hawā*). It is difficult to accept such suggestions. The reason is simple: on what basis are you prefering an opinion of the other school? What are your rules of interpretation (assuming you are a great jurist) or technical standards on the basis of which you are carrying out the selection? Do you believe that *istiḥsān* is valid or not valid, and so on? If you have made a new operating system in which everything works, then that is marvellous. Making a new operating system means you have set up a new school of Islamic law that has unique principles of interpretation. You have then turned into a *mujtahid muṭlaq* like the founders of the schools. In such a case, you do not have to choose, you must undertake fresh *ijtihād* for that is binding on you. And, you must declare the whole set of your principles of interpretation.

Selecting a whole new set of principles of interpretation is the real reason why we cannot have a *mujtahid muṭlaq* today. Maybe, a whole body of scholars can get together and set up a new system. The risk is that no one will follow them. Many modern scholars dream about introducing some kind of reform in Islamic law, and keep on making different suggestions. What they really need to do is to set up a new school. In our view, however, true reform will arise from within the established schools when we have mastered their rules; it cannot be done by breaking school boundaries.

Consequently, in our view, floating between schools, or picking and choosing from different schools amounts to blind *taqlīd*. It is quite different from *taqlīd* that is permitted, and which we will discuss below. The method of *talfīq* (or manufaturing a new opinion from parts of different rules of different systems) is even worse. We will have to return to these topics again when we take up the discussion of *fatwās*.

CHAPTER 3

TAQLĪD AND ITS IMPLEMENTATION WITHIN THE SCHOOL

Taqlīd, as generally understood, means following the opinion of the schools of Islamic law in matters of conduct. Thus, a Ḥanafī follows the opinion of the Ḥanafī school, while a Shāfi'ī follows the opinion of the Shāfi'ī school. As opposed to this, *ijtihād* means that the person in need of an opinion does not follow the opinion of any school, but derives the rule of conduct for himself directly from the sources of Islamic law. Such a person would obviously be designated as a *mujtahid*, and the *mujtahid* must have some basic qualifications. Further, the *mujtahid* must follow a system of interpretation: either an established system of a school or one that he has devised for himself, which will mean a new school. All persons who cannot lay claim to the status of a *mujtahid*, due to the lack of requisite qualifications and skills, must follow the opinion of some *mujtahid*, that is, they must perform *taqlīd*. Yet, we find that in modern times many scholars have condemned *taqlīd*, and have insisted on the necessity of *ijtihād*.

The reason for this is that in the writings of some of the earlier jurists *taqlīd* is considered mandatory for all jurists and independent *ijtihād* is not permitted. This is also termed as the "closing of the gates of *ijtihād*." There have been many discussions on this issue in modern *fiqh* literature, probably started by scholars like Rashīd Riḍā of Egypt. In the light of these discussions, many modern scholars maintain that the doors of *ijtihād* were never closed and this activity should be carried on in the modern world, and *taqlīd* should be shunned. Do these scholars mean that every layman should interpret the sources of Islamic law for himself and should avoid following the opinions of the schools of law? Do they mean that some scholars should undertake *ijtihād* and the rest should follow their opinions? In reality, many scholars have adopted this course, especially the Islamic televangelists.

There is another form of *taqlīd* too, in which a layman does not follow one school, but chooses whichever opinion he likes from one of the schools. Thus, a scholar may choose an opinion from the Ḥanafī school today and tomorrow he may choose one from the Shāfiʿī school or from some other school for that matter. Is this *taqlīd* or *ijtihād*, or is it something else? We have already stated in the previous chapter that this is not proper.

Our purpose in this chapter will be to explain the exact meaning of *taqlīd* as it is understood by the jurists. This will be followed by the methods or structure through which this permitted form of *taqlīd* is implemented within a school.

3.1 The Meaning and Implications of *Taqlīd*

As compared to *ijtihād*, the purpose of *taqlīd* is to lay down a methodology for the *faqīh* for discovering and applying the law in the light of the already settled law. This is the function of the modern judge too, who discovers the law from the statutes and precedents to settle the disputes brought to him. It is not the task of the judge to legislate or lay down new law in his judgements. Does the modern judge perform *taqlīd* too?

3.1.1 The Literal Meaning of *Taqlīd*

The word *taqlīd* is derived from *qalādah*, which means an ornament tied around the neck (like a necklace) or it is the strap that holds the sheath of the sword and is usually swung around the shoulders. The word *qalādah* is also used to mean the strap by which a piece of wood is hung from the neck of an animal; it prevents the animal from running astray, because it strikes it on the knees when it tries to run. In this sense, the word *taqlīd* carries a restriction within it, and this restriction is found in the technical meaning of the term.

3.1.2 The Technical Meanings of *Taqlīd*

In its technical sense, *taqlīd* is defined by Ibn al-Ḥājj as "acting upon the word of another without *ḥujjah* (proof or lawful authority)." There are two ways in which this definition has been understood, and has led to some confusion about the meaning and role of *taqlīd* in the present times.

The first meaning is assigned by modern writers. Abdur Rahim, for example, understands it to mean the following of the opinion of another without knowledge or authority for such opinion. In other words, when a person asks a jurist for an opinion, he should not ask him about the basis for his opinion, whether it has been derived from the Qur'ān, the *Sunnah* or *ijmā'* or some other source; he should follow it without question. This meaning is accepted generally by most modern writers, and it is this form that they condemn. The earlier jurists do not understand the meaning of the definition in this way.

According to the earlier jurists, the word *ḥujjah* means permission given by the *sharī'ah*. *Taqlīd*, therefore, means following the opinion of another when the *sharī'ah* has not given permission to do so. This meaning makes *taqlīd* unlawful, that is, whoever follows the opinion of another without permission of the *sharī'ah*, is committing an unlawful act.

Following the opinion of a jurist does not fall within this meaning of *taqlīd*. The Muslim jurists maintain that following the opinion of a qualified jurist is permitted by the *sharī'ah*, and is not *taqlīd*. This means that there are two types of *taqlīd:* prohibited *taqlīd* and permitted *taqlīd*. To understand this thoroughly, the *ḥukm* of *ijtihād* as well as that of *taqlīd* needs to be examined.

To understand the meaning of *taqlīd* in law, let us examine the definition again. According to the jurists, the use of the word *ḥujjah* in the definition, "acting upon the word of another without *ḥujjah*," excludes this activity from the meaning of *taqlīd*. Al-Shawkānī explains that the use of the word *ḥujjah* excludes the following four types of activity from the meaning of prohibited *taqlīd:*

- Acting upon the words of the Prophet (peace be on him) is not prohibited *taqlīd*.
- Acting upon *ijmā'* is not prohibited *taqlīd*.

- Acceptance of the word of an upright (*'adl*) witness by the *qāḍī* is not prohibited *taqlīd*.

- The layman acting upon the word of a jurist is not performing prohibited *taqlīd*.

The Ḥanafī jurists may add a fifth case to this: acting upon the opinion of a Companion of the Prophet is not prohibited *taqlīd*. These cases do not fall under condemned or prohibited *taqlīd*, because the *sharī'ah* has permitted all these forms; a *ḥujjah* (proof) exists for such permission. Some of these cases are obvious, but the case of the *faqīh* is explained by al-Ghazālī as follows:

> If it is said that you have condemned *taqlīd*, and this (layman's *taqlīd* of the jurist) is the very essence of *taqlīd*, we shall respond that *taqlīd* is the acceptance of an opinion without *ḥujjah*, but following the opinion of the *muftī* has been made obligatory (*wājib*) for the layman through the *dalīl* (evidence) of *ijmā'*, just as it is obligatory for the judge to accept the statement of (an *'adl*) witness.

The authority permitting this activity, and excluding it from the meaning of *taqlīd* is *ijmā'*. Following the opinion of the jurist by the layman, therefore, cannot be called prohibited *taqlīd*, that is, condemned *taqlīd*.

Some jurists exclude some more cases from the meaning of condemned *taqlīd* on the basis of the principle of necessity (*ḍarūrah*). The founder of the Mālikī school, Mālik ibn Anas, is said to have permitted fourteen cases of *taqlīd*. A few of these are given below:

- It is permitted to the layman to accept the opinion of a doctor (*ṭabīb*).

- It is permitted to accept the opinion of a trader in the valuation of property (as an expert).

- The buyer is allowed to accept the opinion of the butcher that the meat he is buying has been properly slaughtered.

- The statement of a child bringing permission to the guest at the door that he is allowed to enter may be accepted by the guest.

This shows that *taqlīd* is a part of our daily lives and we are indulging in some form of *taqlīd* at each step. The truth of this claim is driven home when we examine our modern legal system.

3.1.3 *Taqlīd* in the Pakistani Legal System

The Constitution of Pakistan deems *taqlīd* obligatory in articles 189 & 201. These articles make the judgements of the Supreme Court binding on all courts and the judgements of the High Courts binding on courts subordinate to them. The doctrine of precedent and *stare decisis* are nothing more than institutionalised forms of *taqlīd*. When the lower courts follow the opinions of the higher courts they are undertaking *taqlīd*.

In addition to this, laymen accept the opinions of lawyers in their daily legal problems. Likewise, the courts accept the statements of witnesses, unless their veracity is challenged. The opinions of experts are accepted in a host of other matters.

The conclusion we may draw from this is that *taqlīd* is an essential principle of our daily lives and is based upon division of labour where some persons specialize in certain areas and become experts. The *muftī* or the *faqīh* is an expert in his area and there should be no hesitation in accepting his opinion by those who are laymen in his field of specialization.

3.2 The Primary Function of a School of Law

In the Islamic legal system, the system of *taqlīd* or following precedents is implemented through the schools of law. The primary function of the school is, therefore, to make the law clear and evident for the people who follow the school, whether these are individuals, institutions or the rulers themselves.

One often hears people complaining that the Muslim jurists disagree about everything. There are multiple opinions in the school and one does not know which opinion to follow. These views are not expressed by laymen and students alone; one hears even some teachers saying this and the fact is reflected in their method of teaching as well. In other words, they indulge in what is called *qīla wa qāla*, that is, this jurist said this and the other said that, and yet another said something else.

How then can a person following a school know what the law is? Answering this question is the primary function of the school. From the multiple views existing within the school, a single opinion is preferred. The preferred opinion is the law. In fact, there is a special class of jurists who are assigned this function. They check many things including the sound narration of views within the school. In cases where there is some confusion, the school will issue a *fatwā* upholding one of many opinions as the law to be followed. It is due to this that one hears the phrase: the *fatwā* today is on such and such opinion.

The rule for this activity is well settled and has been observed for centuries by the school. In fact, this has been done from the very earliest times when the school started maturing. The rule is: there will always be a single **preferred** opinion within the school.

Ibn 'Ābidīn states this as follows:

> The preferred opinion of the school is to be followed, and the opinion not preferred is to be treated as non-existent (*al-marjūḥ ka'l-'adam*). It is as if the preferred opinion has abrogated the other opinions.[15]

There is, thus, no confusion about which opinion of the school is to be followed. This also sets aside the objection raised by some that there are so many opinions in Islamic law that one does not know which opinion to follow. The schools bring uniformity into their law through this method. The method through which the preferred opinion of the school is declared is discussed below.

15. Muḥammad Amīn Ibn 'Ābidīn, *Sharḥ 'Uqūd Rasm al-Muftī* (Karachi: Maktabat al-Bushrā, 2009), 8; Ibn 'Ābidīn, *Ḥāshiyah,* 176.

3.3 The Resources of the School: Jurists, Issues and Texts

The resources of a school of Islamic law are visualized in three hierarchies. There is a hierarchy of jurists, a hierarchy of issues and a hierarchy of texts. An understanding of these hierarchies provides a deep understanding of the structure and nature of a school of Islamic law. In this section, we will look at each hierarchy.

3.3.1 The Hierarchy of Jurists Within a School

The founder of a school has two functions: he lays down the *uṣūl* or the principles of interpretation and he uses these principles to settle the issues of the law (*furū'*). Thus, Abū Ḥanīfah laid down the principles of interpretation for the Ḥanafī school and he used these principles to derive the detailed rulings of the substantive law. The founders of the other schools did the same for their schools. This type of jurist is called the *mujtahid muṭlaq* or the absolute jurist. This jurist is completely independent insofar as he does not indulge in any type of *taqlīd*.

As compared to the founder, there are other jurists who are well qualified to undertake *ijtihād*. These jurists, however, follow the principles of interpretation laid down by their teacher. They use these rules of interpretation to derive the substantive law, and their opinions in this area may differ from those of their teacher. These jurists are performing *taqlīd* when they follow the opinion of their teacher about the principles of interpretation. This type of *taqlīd* is called *taqlīd fī al-uṣūl* or *taqlīd* in the principles of interpretation. The jurist who performs *taqlīd fī al-uṣūl* is called *mujtahid fī al-madhhab* or the *mujtahid* who is independent within the school.

There are other jurists in the school as well who are well qualified, but have not been granted the status of *mujtahid fī al-madhhab*. These jurists perform only one type of *taqlīd*, and this is called *taqlīd fī al-furū'* or following the decisions of the jurists of the higher grade. These jurists follow the opinions or decisions of the school laid down by the *mujtahid muṭlaq* and the *mujtahid fī al-madhhab*.

In a developed legal system, it is not possible that there be just two or three types of jurists. There are several types, and each developed school has determined the grades of the jurists based on these types. It is through these grades that Islamic law implements its system of following precedents. Ibn 'Ābidīn lists these grades for the Ḥanafī school as follows:[16]

1. **The first grade:** *mujtahid muṭlaq* or *mujtahid fī al-shar'*. The *mujtahid muṭlaq* who is the founder of the school, that is, Imām Abū Ḥanīfah. He laid down the principles of interpretation for the school. We have already examined these principles in all the previous modules. The *mujtahid muṭlaq* uses his principles of interpretation to derive the law from the sources (for the *mujtahid*). In short, this type of independent jurist lays down the principles of interpretation as well as the law. He is the absolute *mujtahid* who does not perform *taqlīd* in either of its two forms.

2. **The second grade:** *mujtahid fī al-madhhab* or the *mujtahid* within the school. The *mujtahid fī al-madhhab* performs *taqlīd fī al-uṣūl*, that is, he follows the principles laid down by the founder of the school, and using these principles derives the law himself. His opinion in the derived law may differ from that of his teacher. Jurists like Abū Yūsuf and Muḥammad al-Shaybānī are within this grade in the Ḥanafī school. They used the principles determined by Abū Ḥanīfah to derive the law. In the case of *muzāra'ah* (tenancy), for example, they differed with their teacher. Abū Ḥanīfah declared tenancy to be illegal, while the two disciples (*ṣāḥibayn*) declared it legal. The opinion preferred by the school is that of the *ṣāḥibayn*. The jurists in this grade are independent in all respects, except the *uṣūl* (principles of interpretation).

3. **The third grade:** *mujtahid fī al-masā'il* or the *mujtahid* for new issues. The *mujtahid fī al-masā'il* determines answers to cases that are not settled by the jurists of the first two categories.

16. Ibn 'Ābidīn, *Ḥāshiyah*, 179–80;Ibn 'Ābidīn, *Rasm al-Muftī*, 10–12.

In the Ḥanafī school, jurists like al-Khaṣṣāf, al-Ṭaḥāwī, al-Karkhī and al-Sarakhsī are placed in this grade. *These jurists cannot overturn the cases that have been settled by the jurists of the first two grades. Their function is said to be the determination of new unsettled cases.* Al-Dabbūsī is not mentioned in this category or in any other, but we feel that he might have been on the top of the list in this category.

4. **The fourth grade:** *aṣḥāb al-takhrīj* or those jurists who clarify the law of all the existing cases. The great jurist Abū Bakr al-Jaṣṣāṣ is placed in this category. The truth is that he was no less than any of the jurists in the previous category, and the methodology used by him was the same as that used by the *mujtahid fī al-masā'il*. This category of jurists relies on the principles established by the jurists of the first three grades and extend the law to cases covered by these principles. Their function is more like the modern judge who is said to discover the law and not to lay it down.

5. **The fifth grade:** *aṣḥāb al-tarjīḥ* or those who prefer the stronger opinions in the school so as to bring uniformity into the law. Jurists like Abū al-Ḥusayn al-Qudūrī, al-Kāsānī, al-Marghinānī (the author of *al-Hidāyah*) are placed in this grade. They rely not only on the strength of the argument but also on the narration of the issues from the earlier jurists (see below).

6. **The sixth grade**. The rest of the well known jurists in the Ḥanafī school are placed in this grade. They are said to recognise the stronger opinions preferred by the jurists of the previous grade. Most well known jurists like the authors of the authoritative texts (*mutūn mu'tabarah*) would fall in this category. They have the ability to recognize the stronger narrations from the weak, and the ability to recognize rejected opinions, which they do not relate. An examination of their method and their works reveals, again, that they were no less than the jurists in the previous category.

7. **The seventh grade**. This is the category of the pure *muqallids*, who are not able to perform any of the above tasks. Ibn al-Humām placed himself and all the jurists of his times in this category, as in the quotation that has been reproduced later. It is obvious that Ibn al-Humām does not belong to this category; he should be in the sixth grade at least if not higher. There can be no doubt that all the jurists of the present times would be classified in this category, that is, where the title "jurist" can be assigned to them. We find it extremely difficult to classify our judges who man the courts in this category either, as they have no training in Islamic law.

In what is to follow, we may feel the need to alter these grades in order to make them conform to reality. These grades were identified by later jurists according to their own understanding, so there is nothing binding about the details, however, the idea itself is sound.

3.3.2 The Hierarchy of Issues Within a School

Some writers have erroneously stated that *ijtihād* is a source of Islamic law. For the *mujtahid*, it is a process, the effort that he expends, for the derivation of the law. For the *faqīh*, it is the result of the *ijtihād* that is a source, not the *ijtihād* itself. The output or the result of *ijtihād* is the record of the decisions given by the *mujtahid*. It provides the precedents required by the *faqīh*.

In the Ḥanafī school, the first such source are the books called the *Ẓāhir al-Riwāyah* written and compiled by Imām Muḥammad al-Shaybānī. These are followed by others as shown below:[17]

1. *Masā'il al-Uṣūl* or the *Ẓāhir al-Riwāyah*. These are books that record not only the opinions of the leading jurists of the Ḥanafī school, but also those of other leading jurists like Ibn Abī Laylā and al-Awzā'ī. The first book is called *Kitāb al-Aṣl* or *al-Mabsūṭ*. This is the first book on Islamic law, and most

17. Ibn 'Ābidīn, *Rasm al-Muftī*, 19;Ibn 'Ābidīn, *Ḥāshiyah*, 170.

of the opinions recorded there are to be found today in the Ḥanafī school or even in other Sunni schools.

The other books under this heading are: *al-Ziyādāt* (with a huge commentary), *al-Jāmi' al-Ṣaghīr, al-Jāmi' al-Kabīr, al-Siyar al-Ṣaghīr*, and *al-Siyar al-Kabīr*. All these books have been called *Ẓāhir al-Riwāyah* as they represent the most authentic formulation of the school. What we mean by this is that the methodology used in these books is definitely that of the first jurists of the school and these books have come down to us through a continuous narration.

2. *Masā'il al-Nawādir*. These are cases narrated in books other than the *Ẓāhir al-Riwāyah*.

3. The *fatāwā* and *al-wāqi'āt*. These are opinions of later jurists, or the *faqīhs* on cases not contained in the books listed at (1) and (2) above.

The rule for the above texts is that the issues (rules and rulings) in the first category are to be preferred over those in the second and third category, in case there is a contradiction.

The *Ẓāhir al-Riwāyah* were summarised under the title of *al-Kāfī*. It is on this summary that several important works by later jurists were constructed. For example, al-Sarakhsī wrote his famous 30 volume book, *al-Mabsūṭ*, as a commentary on this summary. Abū Bakr al-Kāsānī also relies on it for his *al-Badā'i' al-Ṣanā'i'*. Later books like *al-Hidāyah* by al-Marghinānī rely on the original as well as on later commentaries.

Books in the Mālikī and Shāfi'ī school that can be compared to the *ẓāhir al-riwāyah*, though written sixty to seventy years later, are *al-Mudawwanah al-Kubrā* by Saḥnūn for the Mālikī school, and the *Kitāb al-Umm* written by al-Shāfi'ī himself. The *Ẓāhir al-Riwāyah*, however, are much more extensive.

3.3.3 The Hierarchy of Texts Within a School

The texts of the school are the different categories of works produced by the jurists. In the Ḥanafī school, these are the earliest case books of the school that consist of cases settled by

Imām Abū Ḥanīfah and his colleagues. These were recorded by Imām Muḥammad. Another category is that of the precis or *mukhtaṣars*. These books record the law that is to be followed. A third category that developed later are called the *fatāwā*, which rely on the *mukhtaṣars*, but add additional cases not covered by the *mukhtaṣars*. Commentaries have been written on all three categories of books and may be said to form a separate class. The description that follows is excerpted from the introduction to our translation of al-Marghīnānī's *Hidāyah*. The detailed description may be more useful for those interested in the nature of the texts.

It is well known that the first works on Islamic law are those written by Imām Muḥammad (God bless him).[18] Some of these works were referred to as the *Ẓāhir al-Riwāyah*. Scholars assign several meanings to this term, however, the meaning we are interested in is that the *Ẓāhir al-Riwāyah* are "the preferred rules from among the different narrations of the rules." Imām Muḥammad's works, besides the rulings of Abū Ḥanīfah, Abū Yūsuf and Muḥammad al-Shaybānī (himself), include a large number of other views. The other views recorded are, for example, those of Zufar, Ibrāhīm al-Nakha'ī, Ibn Abī Laylā, Abū Thawr, and al-Awzā'ī (God bless them all). A system of law that presents such a variety of opinions is difficult to follow, unless some rules are chosen for practice. Accordingly, after recording the rulings of different jurists, Imām Muḥammad himself identified some of those rules that were to be followed by the people. These rules were referred to as the *ẓāhir* rules or the rules preferred for compliance. These rules were primarily recorded in *Kitāb al-Aṣl* or *al-Mabsūṭ*. The recording of preferred opinions does not mean that other rulings were not recorded in this book. It is in *al-Jāmi' al-Ṣaghīr*, however, that Imām Muḥammad focused entirely on the preferred rules that were to be followed by the worshipper as well

18. Imām Mālik's *al-Muwaṭṭa'* and *Kitāb al-Āthār* by Imām Abū Yūsuf cannot be treated as books of Islamic law proper. We do not wish to dwell on a list of Imām Muḥammad's works and the details associated with them. These are well known and have been recorded by us in our works on Islamic jurisprudence, and by others in similar works.

as the *qāḍī*. In fact, he focuses mostly on rules that help deal with violations so that a ruling (*fatwā*), or a decision, can be given to one who seeks it. Thus, we do not find a description of *wuḍū'* or *ṣalāt* in *al-Jāmi' al-Ṣaghīr*. According to 'Allāmah al-Lakhnawī (God bless him), he did not mention those rules that were followed day in and day out by every Muslim. The book was directed entirely at practice (of the jurist); the other details could be acquired from *Kitāb al-Aṣl*. *Al-Jāmi' al-Ṣaghīr* was the first summary or précis in Islamic law that listed only those statements of the rules that were to be followed.[19] The second such summary was *al-Siyar al-Ṣaghīr*, also by Imām Muḥammad. The creation of these summaries shows the essential task of a *madhhab* or school of law: the bringing of uniformity into the law by identifying those rules, the *ẓāhir al-riwāyah*, out of a host of rulings, that were to be followed in practice by the school. These early summaries were not very comprehensive, because these were also the early days of the school; it had not acquired sufficient maturity.

The term *mukhtaṣar* appears to have been used for a rule book first by al-Muzanī (God bless him). He died in 264 A.H., and it is possible that such books were written before his time. His *Mukhtaṣar* is usually published with Imām al-Shāfi'ī's *Kitāb al-Umm*. In the Ḥanafī school, therefore, it was natural that al-Muzanī's nephew, al-Ṭaḥāwī, should use the term first.[20] After this, the writing of *mukhtaṣars* became a regular feature, whether

19. *Al-Jāmi' al-Ṣaghīr* was reported by Imām Muḥammad entirely on the authority of Imām Abū Yūsuf. This adds to its strength. Imām Muḥammad based the work on forty *kitābs*, however, he did not make *bābs* or chapters within these *kitābs*. This work was undertaken by Imām Abū Ṭāhir al-Dabbās. As to why this book was recommended for memorisation depended upon the nature of the cases mentioned. These represented some of the core issues settled by the school. According to some jurists, the issues of this book were held in very high esteem and it was deemed necessary that no one be allowed to become a *qāḍī* or permitted to issue a *fatwā*, unless he had understood the issues of this book. 'Allāmah al-Lakhnawī has listed about forty jurists who wrote commentaries on this book, and these are all the well known jurists whose works we study today.
20. His book is called *Mukhtaṣar al-Ṭaḥāwī*.

or not this title was used. Some of the well known *mukhtaṣars* of the Ḥanafī school are the following:

1. *Al-Jāmi' al-Ṣaghīr* and *al-Siyar al-Ṣaghīr* by Imām Muḥammad al-Shaybānī (d. 189 A.H.). These have been described above.
2. *Mukhtaṣar al-Ṭaḥāwī* by al-Ṭaḥāwī (d. 321 A.H.). He begins with the statement that the book contains rules that cannot be ignored or whose knowledge must be acquired. In these *mukhtaṣars*, the chain of transmission of *fiqh* coming down from the earlier Imāms was maintained.
3. *Al-Kāfī* by Ḥākim al-Shahīd (d. 334 A.H.). This was the text chosen by Imām al-Sarakhsī (God bless him) for his 30 volume commentary, *al-Mabsūṭ*. Al-Marawazī created this book by summarising *Kitāb al-Aṣl* and the two *Jāmi's* through the elimination of lengthy narrations and some repetitions.
4. *Mukhtaṣar al-Karkhī* by Imām al-Karkhī (d. 340 A.H.), the famous Ḥanafī jurist, who is also the author of *Uṣūl al-Karkhī*. We have not had the opportunity to examine this book, but jurists often quote it in their works.
5. *Mukhtaṣar al-Jaṣṣāṣ* by al-Jaṣṣāṣ (d. 370 A.H.). He was al-Karkhī's student.
6. *Mukhtaṣar al-Qudūrī* by al-Qudūrī. This was the text chosen by al-Marghīnānī for his own *Mukhtaṣar*. Al-Qudūrī (d. 430 A.H.) ordered the chapters in his book according to al-Ṭaḥāwī's book and not according to Imām Muḥammad's *al-Jāmi' al-Ṣaghīr*. Al-Qudūrī is said to have written a commentary on al-Karkhī's *Mukhtaṣar*.
7. *Tuḥfat al-Fuqahā'* by al-Samarqandī (d. 538 A.H.). He was al-Kāsānī's teacher and his father-in-law. The book is highly organized and a strict application of the term *mukhtaṣar* will exclude it from this category.[21]

21. The Author, however, says that he has brought in additional issues that were not included by al-Qudūrī, and that he has tried to remove the difficulties encountered in studying al-Qudūrī. Further, he has provided the *adillah* (evidences) and arguments in brief.

8. *Bidāyat al-Mubtadi'* by al-Marghīnānī (d. 593 A.H.). This is the *matn* of which *al-Hidāyah* is the commentary.
9. *Al-Hāwī* by Najm al-Dīn al-Turkī (d. 652 A.H.).
10. *Al-Fiqh al-Nāfi'* by Nāṣir al-Dīn al-Samarqandī.

    After this there was an abundance of such texts and what we mention below are just a few of the well known texts.
11. *Al-Mukhtār lil-Fatwā* by al-Mawṣilī (d. 683 A.H.). The commentary on this *matn* is written by *al-Mawṣilī* himself and is called *al-Ikkhtiyār*. This text is used in al-Azhar.
12. *Majma' al-Baḥrayn* by al-Sā'ātī (d. 694 A.H.)
13. *Kanz al-Daqā'iq* by al-Nasafī (d. 710 A.H.).
14. *Wiqāyat al-Riwāyah fī Masā'il al-Hidāyah* by Burhān al-Sharī'ah Maḥmūd ibn Sadr al-Sharī'ah (d. 747 A.H.). As the title shows, it was a summary prepared from al-Hidāyah itself, not only its *matn*. Ṣadr al-Sharī'ah al-Thānī (d. 747 A.H.), the grandson and student of this author, summarised the summary further, calling it *al-Nuqāyah*, and wrote a commentary on it as well.

Some of the texts that are used by the *madāris* for teaching, referred to as the acknowledged texts (*mutūn mu'tabarah*), are those mentioned at (6), (11), (13) and (14). Some add (12) to this list. In the grades mentioned above, these jurists, the authors of the *mutūn mu'tabarah*, are referred to as *muqallids*. They cannot prefer opinions, but have the ability to identify the strong opinions that are to be followed, that is, opinions preferred by those in the higher grades. In our view, preference should be given to *Bidāyat al-Mubtadi'* as the *matn* for teaching purposes and thereafter *al-Hidāyah* should be used as a commentary to understand the rules, as we elaborate below. Further, *Mukhtaṣar al-Qudūrī* is included within *Bidāyat al-Mubtadi'*.

The *mukhtaṣars* listed above and even those that are not listed form a linked chain. Each *mukhtaṣar* borrows from the one that precedes it. In this chain, preference is usually given to those opinions that came first. The attempt being to commence the statement of the rules with the opinions of the earlier Imāms. This conforms with the system of precedents in Islamic law. *In Islamic law, the precedents assigned priority are those that were laid down first and not those that came later.* The reverse order is followed in the common law, with the latest decision being given precedence.[22] The presumption in Islamic law is that the decisions arrived at earlier are closer to the *uṣūl*,[23] while those that came later are to be handled with caution. Those who are interested in this topic may examine the writings of Ibn 'Ābidīn on the subject. This system of precedents attaches significance to chains coming down from the earlier *imāms*, so as to distinguish the authentic from the spurious and the strong from the weak.

There is yet another feature that we consider most important, and to explain it we have to go back to the great Imām (Abū Ḥanīfah) and his disciples. Roscoe Pound, in his five volume work on jurisprudence, quotes from Hamilton's translation of the *Hidāyah* and says that this is the beginning of the case method of studying law.[24] In our view, this was not the beginning of the case method, rather the beginning was made by Imām Muḥammad in his well known books, which in turn reflects the tremendous effort made by the learned Imām and his teachers. It is because of this contribution alone that he is rightly called the greatest (A'ẓam) Imām. Imām al-Sarakhsī after praising the Imām says the following:

> Al-Shāfi'ī (God bless him) is reported to have said, "The people (jurists) are all dependants of Abū Ḥanīfah (God bless him) in *fiqh*." Ibn Surayj (God bless him), who was a leader among the companions of al-Shāfi'ī (God bless him), has reported that a man criticised Abū Ḥanīfah, so al-Shāfi'ī called him and said

22. This is a wonderful topic for research.
23. That is, they were derived by those who had greater knowledge of the evidences, as they were close to the period of the Prophet (God bless him and grant him peace) and were more proficient in the use of *uṣūl* that they had laid down themselves.
24. The introduction of the case method of study in American law schools is attributed to Langdell and Ames.

> to him, "O so and so, you criticise a person to whom the entire *ummah* concedes three-fourths of knowledge when he does not concede to them even one-fourth." The man said, "And how is that?" He replied, "*Fiqh* is questions and responses (through the formation of cases) and he is the one who alone formulated the questions, thus, half the knowledge is surrendered to him. Thereafter, he answered all the questions[25] and even his opponents do not say that he erred in all his answers. When that in which they agreed with him is compared with what they disputed with him, three-fourths is surrendered to him.[26] The remaining[27] is shared by him with all other jurists."[28] The person repented from what he had said.

Whatever the source of this story, its implication is true. The words "questions and responses" means the formulation of cases, actual or hypothetical, for explaining the rules. This is what the Imām did along with his disciples.[29] Without these cases, *fiqh* would not have been understood, neither by the Ḥanafī jurists nor even by those of the Mālikī and Shāfi'ī schools, but that is another story, which is recorded in the next section. It is because of these cases and the associated rules that all jurists are dependants of Abū Ḥanīfah Nu'mān ibn Thābit ibn Zūṭah (God be pleased with him). It is not without reason then that 'Allāmah al-Lakhnawī says: *wa mā adrāka mā Abū Ḥanīfah?*

The way the rules are elaborated in these works through chains of related cases is simply outstanding and highly sophisticated. This method was developed into an art that reached its perfection in the works of jurists like al-Sarakhsī, who added a tremendous

25. That is, settled the cases.
26. One-half for framing the initial cases and another one-fourth for the right decisions.
27. One-fourth.
28. Due to the possibility that he may have issued the correct rulings even in some of these.
29. Those who design cases today, for case studies, know that this is not an easy task.

amount of supporting detail to these cases. Till that time, Islamic law was a practical law solving problems; it needed all this detail. Today, very few people appreciate these cases or even read and benefit from this unique method of elaborating the law. Credit for further organising the cases in the light of the rules must be given to Ḥākim al-Shahīd as well. Nevertheless, great significance was attached to the study of the detailed cases by the earlier jurists. The idea is captured in another story. Abū al-Faḍl Muḥammad ibn Muḥammad ibn Aḥmad, al-Ḥākim al-Shahīd, who was a *qāḍī*, wrote two books: *al-Muntaqā* and *al-Kāfī*. The latter is the précis prepared from Imām Muḥammad al-Shaybānī's *al-Mabsūṭ* and the two *Jāmi'*s. There is no method more powerful than this for the teaching of *fiqh*. It is also the method that dominated the scene for a long time, until the appearance of the literalists.[30]

Ibn 'Ābidīn has given a few words of warning when it comes to consulting later books. His text is reproduced below:

> As you have known the obligation to follow the preferred opinion out of the various opinions...know then that most of the verdicts handed out today by merely referring to the books of the later jurists are not trustworthy, especially the unverified verdicts in books like *Sharḥ al-Nuqāyah* by al-Quhistānī, *al-Durr al-Mukhtār*, and *al-Ashbāh wa al-Naẓā'ir*...for they contain in many cases the preference of a rejected opinion and the preference of that which is the opinion of another school, not preferred by anyone in this school.
>
> The transmission of an opinion may occur in about 20 books of the later jurists and still the opinion may be incorrect as the first jurist has erred and those coming after him have transmitted the opinion from him.[31]

30. The above passages have been reproduced from the introduction to our translation of the *Hidāyah*. Burhan al-Dīn Abū Bakr Marghīnānī, *al-Hidāyah: The Guidance*, trans. Imran Ahsan Nyazee, 4 vols. (Bristol: Amal Press, 2006), vol. 1, xiii-xvii.
31. Ibn 'Ābidīn, *Rasm al-Muftī*, 13.

Ibn 'Ābidīn is trying to tell us that a case should first be traced in the earliest books, and then in the later. When a case is found, it needs to be subjected to verification. This verification means determining the underlying rule. Without tracing the rule employed, the *faqīh* can never be sure how the new case is to be settled. The tracing of the rule is a process that is identical to tracing the rule and *ratio decidendi* from a series of cases in modern law and separating it from the *obiter dicta*. This process is the essence of the methodology of *takhrīj*. The rule once extracted is used to settle the new case. It is also a process that the *muftī* needs to acquire before he can be called a true *muftī*.

3.4 The Integral Bond Between the Four Sunni Schools

There is a saying that was and is current among the Ḥanafī jurists: "The seed of the discipline of *fiqh* was sown by Ibn Mas'ūd (R), irrigated by 'Alqamah (R), harvested by al-Nakha'ī (R), threshed by Ḥammād (R), milled by Abū Ḥanīfah (R), kneaded by Abū Yūsuf (R), baked by Muḥammad (R), and all the jurists partake of this bread".[32] The truth of this statement cannot be denied by anyone. In fact, we would like to add to the following words to this quotation: "And garnished by al-Sarakhsī (R)."

As has already been explained, the schools of Islamic law are not sects; they are systems of interpretation. Each school has its own independent set of principles, which cannot be mixed up with the principles of other schools without causing inner contradictions and analytical inconsistencies. The set of principles adopted by each school is followed by the jurists within the school. It is obvious that the use of another set of principles, of another school, may lead to a different legal opinion on the derived law. Despite these differences, an integral bond exists between the schools both in the area of *fiqh* as well as *uṣūl al-fiqh*. In this section, we will explain the nature of this integral bond or organic

32. Ibn 'Ābidīn (God bless him) quoting al-Ḥaskafī. Ibn 'Ābidīn, *Ḥāshiyah*, 141.

link. The link shows that the schools developed through an initial effort by the Ḥanafī school and later by mutual cooperation of all the four schools.

We may recall from the history of Islamic law that Kufah, a city in Iraq, gradually turned into a centre of *fiqh* and learning. The foundation for this was laid by the decision of 'Umar (R), who sent 'Abd Allāh ibn Mas'ūd (R) (d. 32 A.H.) as a teacher and *qāḍī* for this area. This learned Companion (R) trained a large number of jurists, who in turn produced students many of whom attained great fame. Among these jurists were Alqamah al-Nakha'ī, his nephew Ibrāhīm al-Nakha'ī, Qāḍī Shurayḥ, and Ḥammād ibn Abī Sulaymān.

The founder of the Ḥanafī School was Abū Ḥanīfah Nu'mān ibn Thābit ibn Zūṭah, possibly of Afghan origin. Imam Abū Ḥanīfah was born in Kufah in the year 80 A.H. (699 A.D.) and died in 150 A.H. (767 A.D.). He is also called Imām A'ẓam or the Great Imām. He began his early education in scholastics (*kalām*) and later developed an interest for jurisprudence under the tutorship of his Shaykh, Ḥammād ibn Abī Sulaymān (d. 120 A.H.).

He was a textile merchant by profession and it is said that due to this reason his *fiqh* reflects his practical approach to legal problems. Abū Ḥanīfah was later given the title of the leader of the school of Ahl al-Ra'y. He is reported to have met some Companions (R) as well, foremost amongst them is Anas ibn Mālik. In this sense, he was a Follower of the Companions (R).

Out of the pupils of Abū Ḥanīfah, four are famous; they were: Abū Yūsuf Ya'qūb ibn Ibrāhīm al-Anṣārī (113–182 A.H.), Zufar ibn Hudhayl ibn Qays (110–158 A.H.), Muḥammad ibn al-Ḥasan ibn Farqād al-Shaybānī (132–189 A.H.), and Ḥasan ibn Ziyād al-Lu'lū'ī. Through these disciples, the fame of the Ḥanafī school spread far and wide. Abū Yūsuf was appointed judge in Baghdad and later became the Chief Qāḍī with authority to appoint judges all over the kingdom. He, thus, had the opportunity to propagate the school of the great Imām.

Muḥammad ibn al-Ḥasan al-Shaybānī, who must have been 18 years old when Abū Ḥanīfah died, takes the credit for recording not only the first books of the Ḥanafī school, but also those of the entire Islamic legal system. The books written by him were of two types: the first were called *ẓāhir al-riwāyah* or books of the primary issues, while the second were called *al-nawādir* or unusual cases. In addition to the above, he wrote *Kitāb al-Ḥujjah 'alā Ahl al-Madīnah,* a book on the use of traditions, and another book on traditions called *al-Āthār.* His version of Mālik's *Muwaṭṭa'* is also considered highly reliable. Abū Yūsuf also wrote a book on traditions called *al-Āthār,* and his *Kitāb al-Kharāj* is very well known. The above books form the foundation of Ḥanafī *fiqh.*

The distinctive feature of Imām Muḥammad's books and hence those of the Ḥanafī school is that they record *fiqh* in the form of issues and cases. Some of these were what are called hypotheticals in law schools today. Hypotheticals are carefully prepared cases for imparting instruction. Imām Abū Ḥanīfah is credited with the creation of all the issues and cases, which run in hundreds of thousands. It is obvious that some of the cases had come down from his teachers, while others must have been brought up by his able disciples. Nevertheless, the arrangement, refinement and organization of these cases is the work of this great jurist, due to which he earned the title of Imām A'ẓam.

It is these cases and issues, and the related case-method, that has led to the development of *fiqh* and Islamic law. They were deemed so important that jurists not belonging to the Ḥanafī school also latched on to them and tried to give their own views according to the principles of interpretation preferred by them. To understand this process and how the link was established we may briefly note some points about how the development of the law took place.

1. The law as we know it today (and by that we really mean today) began to crystallise around the year 100 AH. It became an organized and mature system by the year 132 AH when the Ummayyads lost power. It was the Ḥanafīs who had developed this law. The other schools had not even come into existence as yet.

2. Imām Abū Yūsuf, as the Chief Justice of the Abbasids, and companions collaborating with the rulers refined the system

and recorded the opinions not only of their own school, but those of other well known jurists as well like al-Awzā'ī, Ibn Abī Laylā and others.

3. The development of the other schools followed over the next two centuries. The Mālikī school emerged into prominence with the writings of Sahnūn, while Imām al-Shāfī's school was given some shape by al-Muzanī. This happened one hundred years after Imām Abū Ḥanīfah's death in 150 AH.

4. Schools like those of al-Tabarī and the Ẓāhirīs became extinct.

5. The Ḥanbalī school became extinct, but was revived by Ibn Taymiyyah and Ibn Qayyim towards the middle of the 8th century of the Hijrah.

6. The sound compilations of traditions, like the *Ṣaḥīḥ* of Imām al-Bukhārī, started appearing almost one hundred and thirty years after finalization of the law of the Ḥanafī school.

7. The first compilation of traditions is that by Imām Mālik. The first book on *uṣūl al-fiqh* was written by Imām al-Shāfi'ī. *Qawā'id fiqhiyyah* was written by al-Karkhī, although these were derived from the writings of Imām Muḥammad. Other compilations of these *qawā'id*, it is said, existed much before that.

8. The "theory of interests" or the purposes of the law started emerging a little before al-Ghazālī's time and was fully developed by him.

9. The sixth and the seventh centuries were a period of great creativity. Some say that it was in these centuries that *taqlīd* set in. This is not true.

10. Some of the most powerful works were produced by the jurists of what are now called the Central Asian States.

The truth is that most of the earlier authoritative books of the other schools are a response to what is recorded in Imām Muḥammad's books. *Al-Mudawwanah al-Kubrā* of the Mālikī school compiled by al-Saḥnūn is a response to the rulings given in the above books. Much of al-Shāfi'ī's work is also in response to these works. Imām al-Shāfi'ī, it is well known, stayed with Imām Muḥammad and acquired knowledge from him. This is reflected in his books where he refers again and again to the decisions of the Ḥanafī school, even when he disagrees with them. On many occasions, one finds him disagreeing with Abū Ḥanīfah, but adopting the views of the other jurists of the Ḥanafī school, especially those of Zufar. The Mālikī work *al-Mudawwanah al-Kubrā* expressly acknowledges that they are giving their own views on the Ḥanafī (Iraqi) cases. The figure below shows this link along with the dates of devolopment. We may list these points as follows:

1. The Hanafi School, as already explained, was the first to develop the law systematically on the basis of what they had inherited from the Companions and their students in the form of issues or cases.
2. The Ḥanafī school, with the exception of the Imām, worked in collaboration with the rulers. In some periods, such collaboration decreased, but it did continue in one form or another right up to the time of the Ottoman Turks. Accordingly, this is the school most experienced in the administration of justice.
3. An examination of the earlier sources of the other schools shows that they developed in reaction to, or in response to, the work done by the Ḥanafī school by giving rulings on the issues recorded in Imām Muḥammad's works. It is said that Imām al-Shāfi'ī had memorised the entire *Kitāb al-Aṣl*. There is a constant reference to the Ḥanafī school in his works. In the case of the Mālikī school, *al-Muwaṭṭa'* is the first book to be written by any Muslim jurist, but it is not really a manual of *fiqh*. The first authoritative book of this school is *al-Mudawwana al-Kubrā* written by Saḥnūn. This book expressly mentions that it contains the rulings given by

Ibn al-Qāsim on the issues raised by the jurists of Kufa, that is, the Ḥanafīs. These rulings were issued according to the principles of interpretation adopted by the Mālikī school. The Ḥanbalī school developed by borrowing from all three schools.

THE ORGANIC LINK BETWEEN THE SCHOOLS OF FIQH

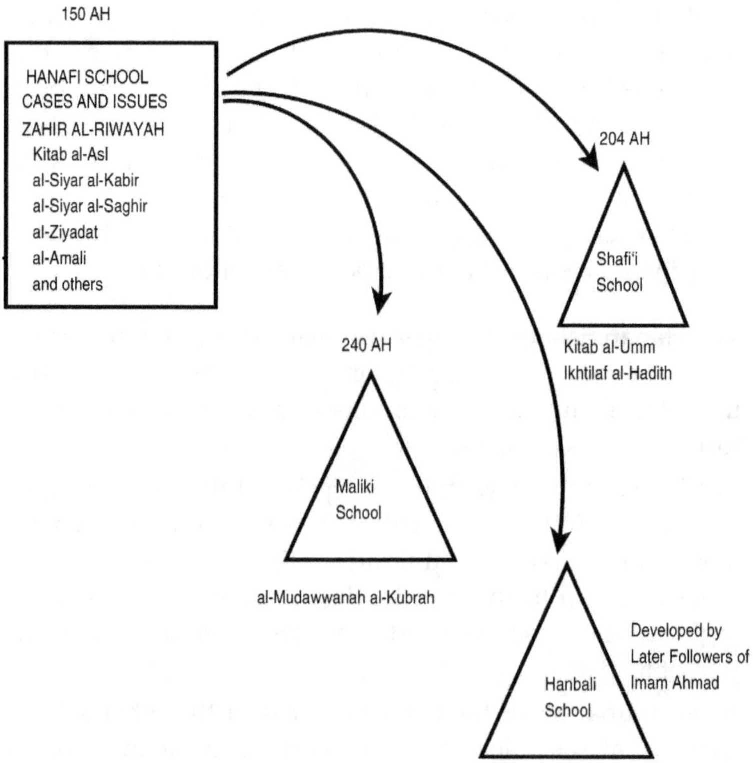

Similar developments can be shown for *uṣūl al-fiqh* as well, and anyone who has read module I carefully must have noticed this. Although it was Imām Shāfi'ī who wrote the first book, the contributions of Ḥanafīs like Jaṣṣāṣ and al-Dabbūsī cannot be overlooked. It was Jaṣṣāṣ who really developed the concept of *bayān* in the light of the views of his teacher al-Karkhī, although we attribute the origin of the idea to Imām al-Shāfi'ī. It was al-Dabbūsī who really organized the discipline of *uṣūl al-fiqh* and set a pattern that is followed by all later books, even till today.

The conclusion we may draw is that the four Sunnī schools are actually like one large family, although they now live in separate houses due to the different set of rules of interpretation adopted by them. These rules are so crucial that people from one house can visit other houses, but cannot stay there or borrow from them. They can, however, move to the other houses permanently if they like.

A word of caution is necessary here. By showing a very close bond between the schools, are we saying that all the four schools are equally valid renditions of the law and we may freely move among them whenever we like? The answer is: certainly not! The only conclusion is that if one moves "completely" to another school there is no problem and he can do so, whether this person is a jurist or a layman. As for the rest of the implication in this idea of "equally valid," the reader will have to wait till we reach the topic.

CHAPTER 4

SEPARATING THE *MUJTAHIDS* FROM THE NON-*MUJTAHIDS*

In this chapter, we will try to assess some of the descriptions provided by the later jurists about how *taqlīd* works within a school. In fact, we will question some of the assertions so that we can arrive at a better picture.

4.1 The Necessity of a School

The great Ḥanafī jurist al-Dabbūsī says that *taqlīd* is the "capital sum" of the ignorant, who does not make an effort due to his inherent "laziness" to learn how to undertake *ijtihād*, because potentially he can if he acquires the skills. This laziness, which we translate as the necessity or need for specialization, led the earlier jurists to create systems through which *'ilm* would be preserved and the need of the ever increasing Muslim population for guidance would be met. He explains the situation as follows:

> The people in the first generation, by which I mean the Companions, their Followers, and the virtuous, may Allah be pleased with them all, based their actions on a *ḥujjah* (legal proof). They used to acquire this from the Book, then from the Sunnah and thereafter from the views of those who followed the Messenger of Allah (pbuh), and these were views validly based on a *ḥujjah*. Thus, one person would adopt the view of 'Umar (God be pleased with him) on an issue, thereafter he would go against this on the basis of the view of 'Alī (God be pleased with him) in another issue. It is proved and firmly established that the companions of Abū Ḥanīfah (God be pleased with him) agreed with his view at times and would oppose it on other oc-

> casions in accordance with what became apparent to them on the basis of a *ḥujjah*.
>
> The school (in these times) was not that of 'Umar (R) or of 'Alī (R), rather the atrribution was all to the Messenger of Allah (pbuh). These were the generations that were praised by the Prophet (pbuh) as those most entitled to blessings. They used to look towards the *ḥujjah* and not towards their *ulamā'* or towards their personal convictions. It was in the fourth generation, when *taqwā* began to fade away from the general public, and the people acquired an inherent laziness in seeking a *ḥujjah*, that they deemed their *ulamā'* as the *ḥujjah*. They began following them and some became Ḥanafīs, some Mālikīs and some Shāfi'īs, thus identifying the *ḥujjah* as human beings. The validity of such a belief came to rest in their being born in a particular school. Thereafter, each following generation followed its own *'ālim* in whatever way they identified him without making distinctions so much so that the earlier practices were converted into innovations and the truth was lost amidst desires.

This may sound as a complaint and as the condemnation of the formation of schools. Some scholars may be tempted to conclude that he condemned *taqlīd* of all types, even in the case of the law. This will amount to reading him out of context. In reality, he fully affirms three types of *taqlīd*. The first of these is the *taqlīd* of the Prophet (pbuh) and this is based on our reason and the recognition of the miracle. The second is the *taqlīd* where one jurist follows another, because it has appeared to him through reason that the other is more qualifed and knowledgeable. The third is the *taqlīd* that the layman performs when he seeks the view of the jurist, and this too is based on reason as the jurist is recognized to have merit. If this is his view about *taqlīd*, what then is his complaint?

His complaint is about "not seeking the *ḥujjah*" or legal reasoning and accepting a scholar as a jurist without knowing what his legal reasoning is, that is, even if it is up to the mark. In other words, following a face and not the merit in his reasoning; we find this being done very agrressively today. It is obvious that such recognition will come from other jurists and not the layman, who does not understand the reasoning anyway. This is a crucial point and we will come back to it towards the end of this module.

Another cause of his complaint might be, and this is merely our personal view, that he was saying that he has all the abilities of being classified among the jurists of the fourth generation at least, yet has been consigned to the position of a faceless jurist. By fourth generation, he obviously meant the generation of the immediate disciples of Imam A'ẓam, or the one following it. If this is his complaint then it was completely justified and genuine, for he was indeed a mighty jurist. We consider it our solemn duty to acknowledge his greatness here. The Muslim Ummah, and that means all the four Sunni schools, owes a huge debt to him. He looms large in the writings of al-Sarakhsi just he does in the works of Imam al-Ḥaramayn and al-Ghazālī. In our view, he was the real "father" of *uṣūl al-fiqh* as we know it today. It is our considered opinion that *Uṣūl al-Shāshī*, which people study so fondly today, is in reality a summary of his work, but has been attributed to al-Shāshī who lived before his time. Finally, and the reader might have noticed this, he looms large in all the modules of this course.

Moving from this to the point of "laziness" or the inability of each individual to seek the *ḥujjah* himself and become a *mujtahid*, we find that the necessity and need for specialization arose. In fact, even during the time of the Companions (God be pleased with them), people used to seek rulings from them, as is indicated in the above quotation. This need for specialization must have become more acute with an increase in the Muslim population as a result of the spread of Islam into different realms. A large number of jurists were obviously needed to meet this rapidly increasing need, jurists who would ultimately spread far and wide to guide the people about the requirements of the *sharī'ah*. How were these jurists to be trained? What methods of interpretation would they use to derive the rules from the texts of the Qur'ān and the Sunnah? How was a uniformity of method to be maintained so that rulings would not be widely divergent? Such obvious questions must have created an acute need for setting up a system for training jurists and regulating their methods.

We may safely conclude that the foundations of such a system, which was direly needed, were laid when the first group of students gathered around the learned Ibn Mas'ūd (God be pleased with him). These first jurists trained by Ibn Mas'ūd (God be pleased with him) began training others and the chain came down right to Abū Ḥanīfah by whose time some standardized rules of interpretation had already been established. The body of these rules of interpretation adopted or preferred by him, and which we have tried to identify in the previous modules, became the system that was henceforth to be called the Ḥanafī school. It was obviously agreed that those who followed the Imām would abide by the rules of interpretation (*uṣūl al-fiqh*) preferred by the Imam, but they were free to derive rules even when they disagreed with the Imām. This then is what actually happened. The disciples of Abū Ḥanīfah followed his system of interpretation, but they differed with his opinion on a point of the derived law whenever another *ḥujjah* appeared stronger to them or when their own legal reasoning led them to a different rule. We have already traced the reasons for disagreement among these jurists in the previous modules. All these rulings were ultimately recorded by Imām Muḥammad al-Shaybānī, who happened to be the youngest of these well known disciples.

4.2 Preserving the School System

A very important point needs to be recorded here, a point that is often ignored by jurists and those who write about these issues. The beginnings of the Ḥanafī school started with Ibn Mas'ūd (R) and continued up to the time of the recording of the views of the school by Imām Muḥammad (God bless him). This lengthy period spreads over a little more than 150 years. In this period, the jurists who constantly developed and refined the system must have absorbed all the traditions coming down from the Prophet (pbuh). These traditions must have been incorporated into their opinions and woven into the system. It is difficult to imagine that an important tradition of the Prophet (pbuh) having a bearing on the law would have been missed in this long period. While it is theoretically possibile, it appears to be impossible when one considers it from the practical perspective, that they could have missed such important traditions. This conclusion is strengthened by the fact that the jurists of this school accepted even those traditions that are called *mursal*; how then could they have missed traditions with complete and sound chains?

To highlight the above point, the great Ḥanafī jurist and Imam, al-Karkhī, turned the point into a *qā'idah* (principle), because it must have been accepted by the school as a whole. The translated text of the principle is as follows:

> Each report (*khabar*) that conflicts with an opinion of our jurists is to be construed as abrogated or that it has conflicted with a similar report. Thereafter, another evidence (*dalīl*) or a preference on the basis of which our jurists argue for preference shall be adopted or a reconciliatory construction shall be placed upon it. This shall be done in accordance with the nature of the evidence. Thus, if a basis for abrogation is established it shall be construed accordingly, but if there is another basis (of reconciliation) we shall adopt that.

Consequently, according to al-Karkhī, if a tradition recorded a hundred years after Imam Muḥammad's time is proved to be authentic, it will initially be presumed to be abrogated. If not then it will be reconciled with the existing rules if possible. This rule is important and will help us draw certain conclusions later.

Related to this point is another important issue. It can be phrased as follows: What if the jurists coming after Imām Muḥammad's time were at liberty to overturn or overrule the views of Imām Abū Ḥanīfah and his immediate disciples on the basis of traditions recorded much later or on the basis of some other argument? Further, if the jurists were at liberty to overrule the rulings of the earlier Imams, were they also at liberty to overturn the rules of interpretation that form the basis of the school?

If these liberties were granted and the later jurists could overturn or overrule the earlier views of the school, the school would be destroyed and its authority eliminated; in fact, the school would not have appeared in the first place. If they were also at liberty to question and alter the rules of interpretation or the system of interpretation, the very basis of the school would be extinguished and its foundation smashed.

The school, therefore, made another major provision. This move consisted of three things. These are described separately below.

4.2.1 Understanding the Hierarchy of Jurists Within a School

The first step was to regulate the liberties of the jurists on the basis of their skills. A grading of jurists was established, which varies with respect to the number of grades, with some preferring seven grades and others preferring five. These have already been described above, relying on Ibn 'Ābidīn.

We need to analyze this structure to understand it better. The first thing that is obvious is that the complete structure of seven types is the creation of the later jurists. The classification is attributed to Ibn Kamāl Pāshā, who died in the eleventh century of the Hijrah. Many later scholars have raised various objections about this seven-fold classification. What is visible at first glance is that these later jurists are being very cautious and careful in describing the grades. It is the same care that is visible in the statement of Ibn al-Humām recorded below about *muftīs*.

The first point that we would like to make is that most of the jurists in grades three to six were extraordinary jurists. In fact, it would not be wrong to say that they were *mujtahids*. Ibn 'Ābidīn acknowledges this. Almost all of the names mentioned in these grades have produced works of the highest standards, which only a jurist of that status can do. Whoever studies their works with care will reach the same conclusion. All of them may have been willing to accept a lesser status, *but they did this for the sake of the school and for its preservation.* Some scholars have indicated that the title *mujtahid fi'l-madhahb* is a lesser title for the immediate disciples of Abū Ḥanīfah, and that they were full *mujtahids*. For us, this point is not very important, as long as they were following his *qawā'id uṣūliyyah* they were within his school, even if on occasions they attempted to refine these *qawā'id* too. We are more concerned about the system than about individual names. The learned 'Allāmah 'Abd al-Ḥayy al-Lakhnawī has critically analyzed the classification into various grades and has said that they have unjustly placed some jurists in lower grades when in reality they were outstanding jurists and better than many others. His introduction to Ṣadr al-Sharī'ah's commentary on *al-Wiqāyah* is very informative.

The second point to be noted is that the seventh category is too general and is in need of exceptions. The reason is that if the stamp of not being a true jurist is placed on all persons, the activity of reasoning will come to a halt and new issues cannot be settled according to Islamic law. In reality, this in itself may be the cause of doctrines like *talfīq*.

Finally, we conclude that this grading actually emphasized two basic rules:

- *First, that the rulings issued by the Imāms in the first two grades cannot be overturned or overruled.* The reason for this has been identified earlier. These were the jurists who were part of the formation of the principles of interpretation, were involved in the process that absorbed traditions with a legal content in the earlier stages, and applied the rules of interpretation to the texts for the derivation of the rules of law—the formative process that resulted in the first collection of cases and issues. In short, these jurists, as is said, were "closer to the *uṣūl*." Their rulings have to be preserved if the system is to survive and develop. There have been exceptions to this in later times, but they do not affect the rule as a whole. The rule is that one of the opinions of these jurists is preferred, but those that are not preferred are not done away with; they lie waiting.

- *Second, that new issues cannot be settled by every jurist; the jurist who attempts to do this must be skilled in legal reasoning and in the working of the system.* It is for this reason that the grading system places the settling of new issues not considered by the Imāms in the first two grades, immediately after the grades of the earlier Imāms. In our view, jurists of grade three to five were qualified for this task, although there were jurists in the later categories too who could perform the same function.

With this we move to the second step.

4.2.2 Understanding the Hierarchy of the Earlier Rulings

Once the rule had been settled that the rulings of the earlier Imams could not be set aside or overruled, a need was felt to organize the huge corpus of rules transmitted by and from the earlier jurists. The three grades of the *masā'il*, described above, were the result of this rule.

The rule for such texts was that the issues in the first category were to be preferred over those in the second and third category, in case there was a contradiction. The ground was laid for retrieving the authentic narration so that the jurists could know what was to be followed and what was to be turned down.

Most of the books produced have kept this criterion in view for preference and for the verification of the views transmitted.

It may be pointed out here that though many scholars mention the *uṣūl* and *qawā'id* of the Imām, they do not make clear distinctions. It is only from the writings and works of some great jurists that we can identify the distinctions. This is what we have tried to do in these modules.

4.2.3 Understanding the Hierarchy of Texts Within the School

After settling the above rules, the jurists of the school set themselves the task of identifying the most authentic and preferred views of the school to be followed as the law. This was indeed a complex task, for they not only verified the chains of narration coming down to them, but also the strength of each view, the preferrence of a view when there was a conflict and a host of other issues. The later jurists dedicated their lives to this task and the Ummah can never thank them enough for the gift they have bestowed on it through this treasured literature. These texts are the heart of the *muftī*'s work and his expertise depends on how well he has mastered these powerful texts.

4.2.4 The Result of the Three Steps

The three steps outlined above led to what is called the system of *taqlīd* or following precedents. The main aim was to preserve the school and its authority. For doing so, the authorities of the jurists had to be kept under some kind of restraint. A line had to be drawn that could not be crossed and this in reality meant determining what a jurist could overrule and what he could not overrule. In other words, certain precedents were deemed as mandatory and binding. These could not be overruled at all; only a preference between them could be exercised. This is the hidden meaning within all the grades of the jurists. The sanctity of these precedents diminishes gradually as we move down the ladder. Thus, al-Sarakhsi could easily overrule al-Karkhī, al-Jaṣṣāṣ and al-Dabbūsī, but beyond that it was not allowed. The *masā'il al-uṣūl* became untouchable so to say.

Another process was the identification of a single mandatory and binding precedent out of several that could be found in the *masā'il al-uṣūl*. This is the underlying meaning of *tarjīḥ*. The next move was to determine the binding precedents from the works of the later jurists. The *fatāwā* literature emerged in support of the *mukhtaṣars* to handle this issue.

The system then is a clear hierarchy of what law is to be followed as stable law. The primary function of the school is, therefore, to make the law clear and evident for the people who follow the school, whether these are individuals, institutions or the rulers themselves.

The theme of overruling rulings lies at the bottom of the institution of *iftā'* as well and we will have to return to this topic again and again, till such time that the meaning becomes absolutely clear. The framework, however, in which we consider this theme from now on, will be that of issuing *fatwās*.

CHAPTER 5

WHAT IS A *FATWĀ* AND WHO IS A *MUFTĪ*?

The first question we will take up is: who is a *muftī*? This will lead us to the obvious discussion about the situation where the *muftī* is a *mujtahid* and the situation in which he is not. What is the difference between the method of these two types of jurists for deriving the rulings that they issue? What are the sources available to each, and how does he use them? How is the activity of the *mujtahid muftī* affected when he performs *taqlīd* within the school? We will then answer some controversial questions when we reach the present times and the needs of this age, that is, what is the role of the *muftī* today?

5.1 What is a *Fatwā*?

The word *fatwā*, also *futyā*, whose plural is *fatāwā* and *fatāwī*, means "response" to a question of any kind. In the technical sense, it means responding to a question about a *ḥukm shar'ī*. It has been used in the Qur'ān in the general as well as the technical sense. For example, the technical meaning is to be found in the verses: "They ask thy instruction concerning the women: Say: Allah doth instruct you about them,"[33] and "They ask thee for a legal decision. Say: Allah directs (thus) about those who leave no descendants or ascendants as heirs."[34]

Many scholars assign a wide role to the *muftī* or the expert who answers such questions. Thus, they do not confine the responses and questions to purely legal rules, rather they include tenets of faith (*'aqā'id*), traditions, and general matters of religion within his domain. They do this to distinguish his domain from that of the *qāḍī* who does not render rulings about general mat-

33. Qur'ān 4:127.
34. Qur'ān 4:127.

ters or even about *'ibāḍāt*. Making the *muftī's* role all-embracing is likely to confuse matters, therefore, we would like to confine his domain to all that is included in the books of *fiqh*. The reason is that the methodology of the *muftī* revolves around such books and his method of verifying his answers also lies within these books. The maximum that he may be allowed, beyond this, is to issue a ruling on an issue of *uṣūl*, and that too simply for instructional purposes. In other words, a *fatwā* must be confined to matters in which *taqlīd* is valid. Accordingly, *fatwā* may be defined as follows:

> It is an authoritative statement about a *ḥukm shar'ī*, in response to a question, when the ruling has been derived from the acknowledged sources of the school and is in conformity with the *uṣūl, qawā'id* and precedents adopted by the school. When no precedents are found in the sources of the school, it is an authoritative ruling issued in the light of the sources of Islamic law maintaining conformity with the *uṣūl, qawā'id* and general propositions adopted by the school.

The word *ḥukm shar'ī* obviously includes the *ḥukm talīfī* as well as the *ḥukm waḍ'ī*. The term "general propositions" are used in the sense of general rules or principles, whether these are to be found in the texts or are implied by them and have been derived by jurists in the form of general principles. This, then, can be a working definition and it is obvious that further refinements may be desired.

The methods for deriving the authoritiative statement, about the *ḥukm shar'ī*, have been discussed at length in the previous modules. The person who is able to use the methods described there definitely possesses the basic qualifications to derive the rule. Nevertheless, some additional requirements are imposed by jurists, and rightly so, which this person has to meet to be able to issue *fatwās*. We will deal with these additional qualifications towards the end of this module.

In certain cases, a person who does not possess the requisite qualifications for issuing a *fatwā* may be permitted to do so by the system due to necessity. If he is not permitted, and there is no qualified person available, the people will not be able to receive necessary guidance. Accordingly, many of the discussions and debates pertain to the rules for such a person.

5.2 Who is a *Muftī*?

The learned Ibn 'Ābidīn quotes Ibn al-Humām as follows:

قَالَ فِي [فَتْحِ الْقَدِيرِ] :وَقَدْ اسْتَقَرَّ رَأْيُ الْأُصُولِيِّينَ عَلَى أَنَّ الْمُفْتِيَ هُوَ الْمُجْتَهِدُ، فَأَمَّا غَيْرُ الْمُجْتَهِدِ مِمَّنْ يَحْفَظُ أَقْوَالَ الْمُجْتَهِدِ فَلَيْسَ بِمُفْتٍ، وَالْوَاجِبُ عَلَيْهِ إذَا سُئِلَ أَنْ يَذْكُرَ قَوْلَ الْمُجْتَهِدِ كَالْإِمَامِ عَلَى وَجْهِ الْحِكَايَةِ، فَعُرِفَ أَنَّ مَا يَكُونُ فِي زَمَانِنَا مِنْ فَتْوَى الْمَوْجُودِينَ لَيْسَ بِفَتْوَى، بَلْ هُوَ نَقْلُ كَلَامِ الْمُفْتِي لِيَأْخُذَ بِهِ الْمُسْتَفْتِي. وَطَرِيقُ نَقْلِهِ لِذَلِكَ عَنْ الْمُجْتَهِدِ أَحَدُ أَمْرَيْنِ: إمَّا أَنْ يَكُونَ لَهُ سَنَدٌ فِيهِ، أَوْ يَأْخُذَهُ مِنْ كِتَابٍ مَعْرُوفٍ تَدَاوَلَتْهُ الْأَيْدِي نَحْوُ كُتُبِ مُحَمَّدِ بْنِ الْحَسَنِ وَنَحْوِهَا؛ لِأَنَّهُ بِمَنْزِلَةِ الْخَبَرِ الْمُتَوَاتِرِ أَوْ الْمَشْهُورِ انْتَهَى ط.

The text above says that, according to Ibn al-Humām, the view of the *uṣūlīs* has come to be established that the *muftī* is one who is a *mujtahid*. As for the non-*mujtahid*, from among those who memorize the views of the *mujtahid*, he is not a *muftī*. For this (latter) jurist, it is obligatory that when he is asked a question that (in his response) he mention the view of a *mujtahid*, like Imām (Abū Ḥanīfah), by way of narration. Thus, it becomes known that what is termed *fatwā* of the existing jurists (those living) in our times, is not a *fatwā*, rather it is the transmission of the view of the *muftī* (*mujtahid*) so that the questioner may adopt it.

He then goes on to say: The method of transmitting this from the *mujtahid* can be in one of two ways: (1) He should either have a source on which he relies. (2) He should acquire the view from a well known book that is used by jurists, like the books of

Muḥammad ibn al-Ḥasan and others like them, because his transmission is a report like a continuous or well known *khabar*.

The above statement creates huge problems for us in understanding the task of the *muftī* today. Some of the problems arising from the statement are as follows:

1. If a jurist of the stature of Ibn al-Humām is saying, "Thus it becomes known that what is termed *fatwā* of the existing jurists (those living) in our times, is not a *fatwā*, rather it is the transmission of the view of the *muftī* (*mujtahid*) so that the questioner may adopt it," then **it means that there were no *mujtahids* within his school during his times.**

2. Does the above statement imply that a *mujtahid* cannot exist within the school? **It is obvious that this is not the implication.** We will explain this in what follows.

3. If there have been *mujtahids* in the school, but they are confined to the founder and his two disciples, then the *fatwā* transmitted can only be confined to the views of these three jurists. Ibn 'Ābidīn records seventeen cases in which the view of Zufar has been preferred. Does this mean that the views of the later jurists are of no consequence for the issuance of transmitted *fatwās*?

4. If the words "*mujtahid* imām" in the above quotation mean the absolute *mujtahid* or the founder, then, is the transmitted *fatwā* to be confined to the view of Imām Abū Ḥanīfah alone? There are detailed discussions about this issue in the writings of the jurists. We will discuss this issue at length.

5. If there cannot be a *mujtahid* within the school today and those issuing *fatwās* are mere transmitters, **then how are new problems to be solved, because the transmitter does not have the ability to go beyond what is already present?**

6. If new problems cannot be solved then **what is the qualification of people who are giving solutions for all kinds of problems,** beginning with Islamic laws given by states and

ending with Islamic banking, and other similar modern issues under titles like *jadīd fiqhī masā'il*?

These are some of the questions we may raise at this stage. If all or some of the propositions are accepted as true, then, on the face of it, it is a situation of absolute *taqlīd* of the absolute Imām, or it may be relaxed to the case of the absolute Imam and his immediate disciples: two or more. This will prove the truth of the statement that the "gates of *ijtihād* were closed" by later jurists. It is possible to say that Ibn al-Humām, who was a great jurist and some kind of *mujtahid* in our reckoning, was being modest in denying the right of *ijtihād* to himself. Nevertheless, he appears to be denying this right not only to himself but to all others too who were living in his times. If an extreme interpretation is placed on Ibn al-Humām's statement, as already indicated in the above questions, then the right of *ijtihād* is denied even to those jurists who came after Imām Abū Ḥanīfah and his disciples. The entire analysis, taken as a whole, reduces the modern *muftī* to the position of a reproducer of the views of the earliest Imāms and a mechanical transmitter of such views; he has no right of *ijtihād* either for new issues or for the old issues.

Having said that, we need to remphasize that Ibn al-Humām was no ordinary jurist. In fact, he had unique skills and an extraordinary legal mind. There is a hidden wisdom in his statement that must be recognized. Consequently, while resolving the above problems we must constantly search for this hidden meaning.

We, therefore, face an uphill task if we have to provide a method for the solution of new problems. This can only be done if we analyse the entire structure of the school and see how the jurists have been operating. What we have already studied in the previous modules about related issues will obviously prove useful here.

5.3 Recalling the Meaning of *Ijtihād* and *Taqlīd*

We will state at the outset that the difficulties and confusions with which the area of *fatwās* is surrounded cannot be resolved unless reasonable clarity is attained about certain fundamental terms and issues. In the previous modules we have been trying to explain the nature of *ijtihād* and *taqlīd* in different ways. The nature of these concepts must be clearly appreciated before we can attempt to analyze the nature of *fatwās* and associated problems.

The first concept that we have to establish is that there is a body of rules called the *qawā'id uṣūliyyah* from which the discipline derives its name of *uṣūl al-fiqh*. We have tried to list as many of these rules as we could in the previous modules. A school of Islamic law is, in the first instance, based on these *uṣūl*. Most of these *uṣūl* have been laid down by the founder of the school: the Imām A'ẓam in the case of the Ḥanafī school. In addition to this, we have also discussed in great detail another body of rules called the *qawā'id fiqhiyyah*. Many of these have also been preferred by the Imām, but in both types of *uṣūl* the later jurists have provided refinements. We have also shown how legal reasoning employs both kinds of rules in a combined effort to arrive at the rules of action called the *furū'*. The concepts of both *ijtihād* and *taqlīd* revolve around these *qawā'id*. We have found these assertions fully confirmed in the writings of the great Mawlānā Ashraf Alī Thanawī (God bless him). Those who still follow his works will find the ideas scattered all over his writings.[35]

Ijtihād or interpretation of the texts for the legal meaning contained in them is a powerful activity. Nevertheless, it operates at different levels. The first level is that of the absolute or independent *mujtahid*, who has his own *qawā'id uṣūliyyah* and *qawā'id fiqhiyyah*. He derives the *furū'* by using his *uṣūl* and *qawā'id* in a manner that is unrestricted by any constraint. The status of the all powerful *mujtahid* is assigned only to Imām Abū Ḥanīfah for the

35. See, e.g., Ashraf 'Alī Thānawī, *Ijtihād-o-Taqlīd kā Ākhirī Fayslah* (Karachi: Zamzam Publishers, 2004).

Ḥanafī school. It is prohibited for this type of jurist to follow the views of another jurist, because it is obvious that their *uṣūl* will clash leading to contradictions. This too is affirmed by Mawlānā Thānawī.[36]

The second level of operation is that of the immediate disciples or students of the Imām. These were jurists with exceptional talent. In fact, they had the potential of becoming absolute *mujtahids* just like the Imām, but they preferred his method of interpretation to what they would have selected themselves. They agreed to follow the Imām's *uṣūl*, and by doing so they eliminated the possibility of clashes and contradictions. There is no other restriction on this second category of jurists. Thus, they are not bound by precedents laid down by the Imām; they treat every issue as an absolutely new issue. Yet, they are *muqallids* in some sense; their *taqlīd* is *taqlīd fi'l-uṣūl*. Imām al-Ghazālī has stated that they differed with the Imām in at least 25% of the *furū'*.

At the third level, we have jurists who accept not only the *uṣūl* of the school, but treat the *furū'* derived by the first two grades as precedents. There is, however, a secret that needs to be uncovered here. Precedents for these jurists, who in reality have the potential of being independent *mujtahids*, are more like precedents in English common law. No single precedent is binding for them although they may accord more importance to one of the several precedents. On very rare occasions, and this secret too we have discussed at length in the previous modules, they may even differ with the earlier jurists. This liberty is primarily due to the distinctions drawn in the interpretation of facts and not on the basis of *uṣūl* or textual *dalīls*. There is no *taqlīd* in facts, and that is the reason why we have new *masā'il*. Consequently, some liberty is available to interpret facts somewhat differently from the way the earlier Imāms did. Today, someone may reason that the presumption of puberty should be fixed at 16 years rather than 15 or 18, and he may adduce scientific or medical evidence for all this. Nevertheless, the disagreement of these jurists with the earlier Imāms is rare. Insofar as these jurists settle new cases, the

36. Ibid., 20, 70.

legal reasoning they adopt is that of *takhrīj*. The methodology has been described in detail in a previous module on legal reasoning. In simple words, it means reasoning from the principles settled by the earlier jurists to extend the rule of action to new cases. In this category, we would like to place al-Ṭaḥāwī, al-Karkhī, al-Jaṣṣāṣ, al-Dabbūsī, al-Sarakhsī and some other earlier jurists.

The next, or fourth category, is that of later powerful jurists like al-Samarqandī, al-Kāsānī, al-Marghinānī. These great jurists also undertake *ijtihād* of a limited type within the school. Some additional restrictions are voluntarily accepted by these jurists for the sake of the system called the school. The restrictions and liberties may be listed as follows:

- They undertake *takhrīj* for new cases.

- The precedents laid down by the Imāms, in the first two categories, are binding in the sense that they cannot be overturned or swept aside, but one of these precedents can be chosen as binding, just like one option may be chosen out of several in *kaffārah*. The selection is based on many factors, but also on how facts are interpreted in the time of these jurists.

- The precedents laid down by the previous, or third, category through new cases settled on the basis of *takhrīj* are also precedents (see Thānawī)[37] but not binding in the sense that they cannot be overruled or distinguished. This too will be based on a different appreciation of facts in the legal sense.

- It is the jurists of this fourth category too to whom the later jurists apply the term Mashā'ikh. Some of the jurists who came after these jurists may also qualify for this category, for example, Ibn al-Humām and al-Bābartī. 'Allāmah al-Lakhnawī indicates that the term Mashā'ikh may apply to all jurists other than the Imām A'ẓam.

37. Thānawī, *Ijtihād-o-Taqlīd*, 25.

We arrive at the stated conclusions by examining the texts and works of all the above jurists. A few more crucial conclusions follow from the above. The first is that *taqlīd* in reality is that of the *uṣūl* and *taqlīd* in *furū'* varies with the ability of the *muqallid* jurist (see also Mawlānā Thānawī).[38] The second conclusion is that *takhrīj* or reasoning from *uṣūl*, *qawā'id* and principles is the general methodology of all the jurists in the Ḥanafī school; it is not confined to one particular category of jurists. Third, *takhrīj* can never come to an end within the school. If it does, no new issue can be resolved on the basis of Islamic law (see also Mawlānā Thānawī). As Islam is a complete code of life, this last conclusion has to be true. This is similar to al-Shāṭibī saying that *taḥqīq al-manāt* is a form of *ijtihād* that can never come to an end. We will have more to say about this point later.

The last, and fifth, category is of those jurists who may attain a status, which may not be equivalent to those of the Mashā'ikh of the fourth category, but it may enable them to undertake *takhrīj* in a limited sense. This is necessary so that the process of settling new cases and problems continues. It has to be assumed that some such jurists will always be present in the Muslim world in all ages, so that the development of the law does not come to an end. Before attaining this level, every person who studies Islamic law and attains some qualification is an "aspiring jurist," who is not capable of *takhrīj*, yet, but must constantly strive to attain that ability. If he feels confident that he knows the law, although he has not attained the ability of *takhrīj*, he may issue *fatwās* on the basis of transmission, about which we will have to say more in a later chapter.

38. Ibid., 25.

CHAPTER 6

THE *MUJTAHIDS* WITHIN THE SCHOOL AND FOLLOWING THE *QAWL* (OPINION) OF THE IMĀM, ALWAYS

6.1 Identifying the Issue

In the previous chapter we have tried to show that the jurists from grade three to grade six—*mujtahid fi'l-masā'il, asḥāb al-takhrīj, asḥāb al-tarjīḥ* and the authors of the *mutūn mu'tabarah*—were indeed qualified and able *mujtahids*. The proof of their ability and skills lies in their works that have come down to us. A sign of their greatness and commitment to the school is that they chose to accept a status lesser than what they actually deserved.

It is also not correct to assume that the doctrine of the school has been created by the Imam A'zam and his students alone. The jurists who came after them made huge contributions, and it is their effort that completed the total system that is today called the Ḥanafī school. In reality, most of what we have studied in the previous modules is a heritage left by these later jurists. Given below is a list of some of the contributions made by these great jurists:

1. They elaborated the doctrine of the school by linking the rules to the evidences used by the earlier Imāms.

2. They identified, elaborated and refined the *uṣūl* or principles of interpretation used by the Imām and his disciples, including the rules of literal as well as rational construction.

3. They identified the system of interpretation of facts and organized the *qawā'id fiqhiyyah.*

4. They preferred the views that were most important, strong and authentic over those that were lesser in strength and created a uniform body of the law.

5. They created works that the *qāḍīs* and *muftīs* could memorize for the issuance of rulings.

6. They created huge and elaborate works that would serve posterity and become a perpetual reservoir of instruction for all those jurists who were to come later.

7. They resisted all opposition to the doctrine of the school by outside forces and preserved its purity.

8. Finally, they always accepted and formulated rules of constraints that strenghened and brought order into the school system.

In recognition of the contribution made by these jurists, we will give a few illustrations of the freedom and liberty enjoyed by these jurists for making contributions to the corpus of the law.

6.2 The Activity of the *Mujtahids* Within the School

The first example of the contribution made by later jurists is that of *waqf*. The view of Imām Abū Ḥanīfah (God bless him) on this topic are well known. Imām al-Sarakhsī after recording the statements of Imām Muḥammad with respect to the view of the Imām on the issue, says that it was for this reason that he did not devote time to this topic. It was in reality al-Khaṣṣāf and Hilāl (God bless them), two later jurists, who developed most of the details. The point to be made is that it was the later jurists who developed the details of this part of the law. There are some other examples too. This is also an example of an area where the view of the Imām has not been adopted.

Imām Abū Ja'far al-Ṭaḥāwī (d. 321AH) created a unique *mukhtaṣar*, perhaps the first in the Ḥanafī school if the shorter books of Imām Muḥammad are not treated as *mukhtaṣars*. He was the nephew of the famous Shāfi'ī jurist, and companion of Imām al-Shāfi'ī, al-Muzanī, who wrote the first book entitled *mukhtaṣar*. It was, therefore, natural for al-Ṭaḥāwī to follow the same order for topics as al-Muzanī had done. He was asked as to why he moved to the Ḥanafī school, when his teacher and uncle was a Shāfi'ī. His response was: "I found my uncle constantly consulting Ḥanafī books, so I moved to the Ḥanafī school." For a list of the *mukhtaṣars*, please refer to the previous chapter.

The *mukhtaṣar* by al-Ṭaḥāwī is unique in many ways, and we may list some of these points to highlight them:

1. It records the most authentic narrations from the earlier jurists.
2. It deals with certain topics that have not been dealt with even by later jurists.
3. It records the views of Imāms Abū Ḥanīfah, Abū Yūsuf, Muḥammad, Zufar and Ḥasan ibn Ziyād.
4. If there are several views on an issue, he prefers one view, often giving the reason for doing so, and saying, "This is what we adopt."
5. He sometimes prefers the view of Imām Abū Ḥanīfah, sometimes the view of Imam Abū Yūsuf, and at other times (in fact, quite often) the view of Imam Muḥammad.
6. On some occasions, he opposes the view of all three Imāms and prefers the view of Zufar or that of Ḥasan ibn Ziyād.
7. Sometimes he derives a rule on the basis of the views of the Imams on another related issue, when there is no reported view from the Imams.
8. It also happens that on some occasions, he gives up the view of the Imāms and gives his own view on the issue based on his own *ijtihād*, although this is rare.

Here then is one of the most respected jurists of the school breaking out of the category, *mujtahid fi'l-masā'il*, to which he has been consigned by the later jurists; he was much more than that. His role as a traditionist is well known and we need not dwell on that. His books on *shurūṭ* are not only unique, they are simply outstanding. There are different versions of his *mukhtṣars* on the basis of size. Many commentaries were written on the *mukhtaṣar*, the best known being those by al-Jaṣṣāṣ and al-Sarakhsī, which are in four or five volumes.

In later books, we find countless occasions where the view of one of the disciples has been preferred over that of the Imām. Gradually, however, we see certain authors of *mukhtaṣars* recording the views of all three Imams or of two Imams without any preference, that is, on some occasions. This becomes visible even in *Bidāyat al-Mubtadi'* by the author of *al-Hidāyah.*

Imām al-Ṭaḥāwī died in 321 AH. Almost 400 years after his death, we find the author of *Kanz al-Daqā'iq* making a shift in the generally accepted method. His book is a summary of a book written by Ibn al-Sā'ātī (d. 694AH). Al-Nasafī himself died in 710AH. Al-Nasafī records the view of the Imām on most occasions.

About two hundred and fifty years after al-Nasafī, a little over 400 years from our time, the commentator on his book, Ibn Nujaym (d. 971AH), starts a debate that has caused considerable confusion. The details are in the following section.

6.3 Is it Mandatory for the *Muqallid Muftī* to Follow the View of the Imam and no One Else?

The underlying idea of this debate is that if a jurist is a sort of *mujtahid* or has the ability to distinguish between the views coming down to us from the Imams, he may prefer the view that is convincing for him. If the *muftī* of the present times is a pure *muqallid,* the ruling he issues is not even a *fatwā* (please refer to the quotation above from Ibn al-Humām). All he does is transmit the ruling from the Imam, because it is his *taqlīd* that we all perform. Thus, it is obligatory for a *muftī* today to merely transmit the ruling from the Imam.

Ibn Nujaym, commenting on al-Nasafī's text, made some statements that generated a debate that sheds light on the ability of the *muftīs* of our times and the extent to which they are at liberty to issue rulings. Here is a summarized version of what he said:

> If you say: How was it valid for the Mashā'ikh to issue *fatwās* without relying on the opinion of the Imām, when these Mashā'ikh were *muqallids*? I would say: This has been confusing for me for a long time and I could not find an answer to it, except what I have come to understand now from their text and this is as follows: It has been transmitted from our jurists (the Imāms) that it is not permissible for anyone to issue a ruling on the basis of our opinion until he comes to know why we held the opinion. It is reported in the Sirājiyyah that this is the cause of the opposition of 'Assām with respect to the Imām for he used frequently to issue rulings against his opinion, because he did not come to know the *dalīl*, while the *dalīl* of another was apparent to him. He, therefore, used to issue the ruling according to the other view. I (Ibn Nujaym) would say that this was the condition in their times. As for our times, it is sufficient to memorize as is stated in al-Qinyah and other texts. **Thus, the issuing of a ruling on the basis of the opinion of the Imām is valid, rather it is obligatory even if we do not know on what basis he held that opinion.**

To this he adds the following statement: "The result of this is that **it is obligatory for us to issue a ruling according to the opinion of the Imām, even if the Mashā'ikh have issued a ruling that goes against this view (of the Imam).** The reason is that they ruled against it as the condition was not present (applicable) in their case, which is the reliance upon his *dalīl*. As for us, we have to issue a ruling (according to his view) even if we do not rely on his *dalīl*."

To complete the meaning of what has been said, let us add other rules. What if the view of the Imam is not found on an issue? In that case the rule is: first, Abū Ḥanīfah; second, Abū Yūsuf; and third, Imam Muḥammad.

Who are the Mashā'ikh who have the ability to reason on the basis of the Imām's *dalīl*, or the *dalīl* of the other two Imams? We quoted Ibn al-Humām in the first chapter to show that he denies himself and the jurists of his times the ability to appreciate the *dalīls* of the Imāms, or the capacity of some kind of *ijtihād*. Ibn Nujaym, following al-Nasafī, states that Ibn al-Humām had the ability to appreciate the *dalīls* and to prefer views. Consequently, we have to draw a line at Ibn al-Humām, and the Mashā'ikh are then all well known jurists coming before him, including him.

It may be mentioned here that Ahmad Rida Khan Barelvi wrote a detailed article on this issue in his *Fatāwā* and supported the position upheld by Ibn Nujaym, that is, the *fatwā* issued in our times by a *muftī* has to be based on the view of the Imam. We have not been able to ascertain the Deobandi position on the issue, but the understanding we had from some texts of Mawlānā Ashraf 'Alī Thānawī is that it is not always obligatory to follow his view, although this is not a direct statement (reference is to *taqlīd shakhsī*).

Ibn 'Ābidīn, while adding his gloss to *al-Baḥr al-Rā'iq*, in *Rasm al-Muftī* and even in his *Ḥāshiyah*, opposes this view in the strongest of terms. We will not go into details here, but will only record the gist of his argument.

He first states that the incoherence of these views should be evident to whoever examines them. He then quotes al-Ramlī, who says that if it is merely a question of transmission, then transmission is valid from the Imām as well as from jurists other than the Imām. Ibn 'Ābidin, elaborating this statment, says that the meaning is as follows: The Mashā'ikh came to know of the *dalīl* of the Imām, just as they came to know of the *dalīl* of the other Imāms. If they prefer the *dalīl* of the other Imāms and rule against the view of the Imām, then it cannot be assumed that they were not aware of these *dalīls*, and we have to follow their view. He further elaborates that the Mashā'ikh have filled up their books with these *dalīls* and the associated legal reasoning. In comparison, our situation is such that we do not have the capacity to undersand the principles, the method of *takhrīj*, and we do not have that status. It is, therefore, up to us to follow these Mashā'ikh, because it is these jurists who are the followers of the school and who—with the strength of their *ijtihād*—have borne the burden of establishing and refining the school. In short, the Mashā'ikh know better and we should follow them (he goes into a number of details with supporting quotations). **It is only fair to say that the *muftī* in our times must follow the *fatwā* given by the Mashā'ikh.**

We fully agree with Ibn 'Ābidīn on this issue. We will, therefore, raise questions and give arguments that Ibn 'Ābibidīn could have raised with ease but did not due to his usual politeness; he just used to say, "Ponder over this." Our arguments and questions are as follows:

1. The issue we would like to identify is: whether the *taqlīd* we perform is the *taqlīd* of a human being or that of the system. It is what al-Dabbūsī says when he states that people have started following human beings and have forgotten the *ḥujjah* (refer to his statement above). In reality, it is the Imām who asks us to follow the system when he asks us to adopt his opinion when we have identified why he held it. It is only the system that will tell us why he gave a certain ruling. This applies not only to the principles of interpretation, but also to the rules of law. **The truth is that the school or the system belongs to the Imam, so when we are following the system, we are following the Imām.** It is the Mashā'ikh who represent the system.

   In *Uqūd Rasm al-Muftī*, Ibn 'Ābidīn first records an instruction from the Imām to his disciples: "If a *dalīl* appears stronger to you, give a ruling accordingly." Thereafter, he quotes the disciples to the effect that whatever view they have, and which is against the Imām's view, was once Abū Ḥanīfah's view, but which he withdrew later. The idea behind this is that all of the views are actually Abū Ḥanīfah's. He then brings in a statement to the effect that if a jurist retracts from his view, it can no longer be taken as his view. Acknowledging the difficulty of reconciling these statements, he says: "When the Imām has ordered his companions to adopt from any of his views that which appears to them to be based on a stronger *dalīl*, then what they say will be his view; this is because it is based on the *qawā'id* that he established, therefore, he did not move away from the view in all respects." This is exactly what we meant when we said that true *taqlīd* is that of the *qawā'id* or *uṣūl* (also affirmed by Mawlānā Thānawī).[39] In fact, we will go a step ahead and say that even if it was not originally the view of the Imām, it has a family affinity, for it is based on the *qawā'id* established by the Imām. Consequently, it deserves to be preferred by the Mashā'ikh if it has a stronger *dalīl*, as required by the Imām himself.

2. It follows from the above that it was the Mashā'ikh, working within the system, who told us that there was someone called Abū Ḥanīfah, about his merits, the reasons they followed him, the reasons we should follow him and what the Imam himself said. We do not have access to Imām Abū Ḥanīfah except through these Mashā'ikh. It is a whole chain of transmission. It is true that the *masā'il al-uṣūl* have come down to us from Imām Muḥammad's narration, but that makes Imām Muḥammad very important in the chain. The same applies to the Mashā'ikh, for they have an integral relationship with the whole narration.

3. If we are not to follow the Mashā'ikh, then the entire body of literature produced by these Mashā'ikh, and which we so dearly treasure, is reduced to naught. Even the views of Imams Abū Yūsuf and Muḥammad are only relevant when there is no transmitted opinion from the Imām. This becomes more acute when it is stated that there are no true *muftīs* today, only transmitters.

4. If the view of the Mashā'ikh is not to be acknowledged, then what kind of *ijāzah* or authority is being handed down to the present day *muftīs*? The method of issuing *fatwās* has come down from the Mashā'ikh. If they are not handing down

39. Thānawī, *Ijtihād-o-Taqlīd*, 53.

the method of the Mashā'ikh to their students, what exactly are they handing down? If their views cannot be handed down, their authority cannot be handed down either. If it is merely an authority for transmission, then we do not need people trained in the *madāris* or the universities. Any good Muslim, who can read or write, can be handed the *ijāzah* of transmission.

5. If the Mashā'ikh are no longer relevant, then the only books needed are those of the *masā'il al-usul*, the *nawādir* and the *wāqi'āt*. In this modern age, a highly efficient system of questions and responses can be created on the basis of these books for the retrieval of the *qawl* of the Imām, or those of the other Imāms when his view is not available. This database can then be accessed by anyone who needs a ruling. Who will need the *muftīs* then? The truth, however, is that the *muftīs* of this age, if they are not *mujtahids* as claimed by Ibn al-Humām, they are not even qualified to understand Imām Muḥammad's books. A transmission without understanding is not valid, nor can it be acted upon without understanding. The understanding has been imparted to us by the Mashā'ikh.

Our purpose here was to elaborate the meaning of Ibn 'Ābidīn's statement that the incoherence of these views was evident.

The conclusion is that we must follow the Mashā'ikh when they declare an opinion as the preferred opinion within the school, irrespective of whether it was the Imām A'ẓam's view or that of another jurist. And for discovering what the Mashā'ikh have said, the authority stretches upwards from Ibn al-Humām, who may be considered the last of the true jurists. Consequently, the authorities are Imām al-Sarakhsī, al-Kāsānī and al-Marghinānī. We sometimes feel that the modern day *muftīs* do not even read al-Sarakhsī.

6.4 In What Cases is the *Qawl* (Opinion) of the Imām or of the School to be Given Up?

Al-Ḥaskafī says the following in the opening chapter of his book: "If we are asked about our opinions and about the opinions of the rival school, we will say by necessity, 'Our opinions are correct with a probability of our error (in some cases), and the opinions of our rivals are incorrect, with a probability of being correct (in some cases).'" He says later, quoting al-Timartāshī, "Issuing a ruling or a *fatwā* on the basis of a view that is not preferred (*marjūḥ*) is ignorance and the tearing apart of *ijmā'* (consensus); a *mulaffaq ḥukm* (patched up rule) is a nullity on the basis of *ijmā'* (consensus); retracting from *taqlīd* after having acted upon it is a nullity by agreement, and this is what is the chosen rule in the school; and that disagreement (about the *furū'*) is exclusively for the *qāḍī* who is a *mujtahid*, but as for the *muqallid*, his ruling is not to be executed, if this is against his school." In another, place al-Ḥaskafī records a saying attributed to Imām Abū Ḥanīfah (God be pleased with him): "If you come to face a *dalīl* (evidence), form your opinion on the basis of such evidence."

We will first take up this last quotation in the light of what Ibn 'Ābidīn says in his comments. After this, we will discuss one or two points found in the earlier quotations.

6.4.1 "If a *Ḥadīth* is Proved Sound, Adopt it as my View"—Abū Ḥanīfah

The last quotation given above and the saying about a *ḥadīth* being proved sound, as stated in the heading, mean the same thing. The saying has been attributed to Imām Abū Ḥanīfah by some, and to several Imāms by Ibn 'Abd al-Barr and to all the four Imāms of the Sunnī schools by al-Sha'rānī. This is what Ibn 'Ābidīn says. The implication of both statements is that the Imām is saying: If a tradition is proved sound and it goes against my view, adopt the tradition and give up my view. It is probably due to this reason that we find in the books of modern scholars statements like, "Perhaps the tradition did not reach him."

6.4.1.1 Can the Tradition be Adopted?

We have been arguing in these modules that from the time of Ibn Mas'ūd (God be pleased with him), the jurists who followed his method worked on *fiqh* for almost 150 years before Imām Bukhārī's sound compilation was recorded. In this period, they must have constantly searched for traditions to solve new issues and develop the law. They must have absorbed all the traditions and accommodated them into the law for new issues. There is, however, always a theoretical possibility that they might have missed some tradition.

For a sound tradition that may have slipped through the gigantic effort of the jurists for one hundred and fifty years, Ibn 'Ābidīn says: "It is evident that (acting on) this tradition is for one who is skilled in the examination of the texts, who knows the *muḥkam* and the *mansūkh*. If those eligible in the school examine this tradition and act on the *dalīl* (contained within it), the rule is correctly attributed to the school as it has arisen from the permission granted by the founder of the school, because there can be no doubt that if he himself had declared his (earlier) evidence to be weak, he would have retracted from it and followed the stronger *dalīl*. It is for this reason that Ibn al-Humām objected to the *fatwā* of some Mashā'ikh who ruled according to the view of the two Imāms, and maintained that moving away from the view of the Imām is only permitted when his evidence is proved to be weak." This means that it is only the *mujtahid* who has the right to examine this tradition that has passed unnoticed down to later times; the *muqallid* has no authority, or expertise, to examine this tradition for altering the settled *rulings* of the school.

Here we would like to highlight another dimension that appears to have been ignored by Ibn 'Ābidīn. This is the statement of the great Ḥanafī jurist and Imam, al-Karkhī, on the exact same issue. The statement recalled is as follows:

> Each report (*khabar*) that conflicts with an opinion of our jurists is to be construed as abrogated or that it has conflicted with a similar report. Thereafter, another evidence (*dalīl*) or a preference on the basis of

> which our jurists argue for preference shall be adopted or a reconciliatory construction shall be placed upon it. This shall be done in accordance with the nature of the evidence. Thus, if a basis for abrogation is established, it shall be construed accordingly, but if there is another basis (of reconciliation), we shall adopt that.

Here Imām al-Karkhī is giving advice to the *mujtahid* within the school, because the *muqallid muftī* is excluded from this process anyway. He is saying that there are several presumptions in this case:

1. The tradition discovered now has been abrogated;
2. The tradition has already been considered by the Imām and has not been preferred in comparison to another stronger evidence;
3. The tradition has already been reconciled with the existing evidences.

All three presumptions give rise to a fourth presumption that **the Imām or his school has already taken this tradition into account.** These are rebuttable presumptions, which means that they can be overturned only if evidence is adduced to show that the Imām or the school did not come across this tradition and, therefore, did not take it into account. **The onus of proof is on the person, and we assume he is a jurist, who is presenting this tradition as a new tradition not considered by the school.** What Imām al-Karkhī appears to be saying, and we fully agree, is that there is absolutely no way in which a jurist, however knowledgeable, can come up with evidence to show that the tradition was not taken into account. This holds true even if this jurist masters all the *uṣūl*, *qawā'id* and *furū* of the school. The maximum he can do is to attempt to show why it is considered abrogated, not preferred, or reconciled.

Consequently, if anyone today comes up with an authentic tradition and says that "perhaps this tradition did not reach the Imām or his disciples," such a claim has no basis; in fact, it has no meaning. All the traditions have already been taken into account by the school and are included or accommodated, in one way or another, within the established doctrine of the school.

6.4.1.2 If the Tradition is Adopted, the Jurist Must Stay Within His School

It may be assumed for the sake of argument that a jurist who is a *mujtahid* within the school has been able to show that a certain tradition was not followed by the Imām. Even in such a case, this jurist is required to stay within the school; he cannot adopt the view of another school on the basis of the tradition. This topic concerns the issue of picking or choosing an opinion from another school, which is discussed below, but we will address it briefly here.

The learned Ibn 'Ābidīn says: "I would say: Further, it is necessary to restrict this with (the condition) that the opinion should conform to an opinion within the school, because it is not permitted in *ijtihād* to uphold a view that takes him out of the school as a whole, that is, with what our jurists have agreed upon. The reason is that their *ijtihād* is stronger than his *ijtihād*. It is obvious that they adopted an evidence that was preferrable over what he (the Imam) adopted, and which they did not act upon. It is due to this reason that al-'Allāmah Qāsim said with respect to his teacher Ibn al-Humām, the last of the verifiers: 'The discussions of our Shaykh that opposed the school are not to be acted upon.'" He then quoted the learned Qāḍī Khān, "The method of the *muftī* in our times with respect to our companions is that if he (the *muftī*) is asked about an issue that is related from our (earlier) companions in the authentic narrations without any disagreement among them, then he is to incline towards them and is to issue a *fatwā* according to their view. He is not to go against them in his view even if he is an established *mujtahid*. The reason, it is obvious, is that the truth lies with our companions and does not go beyond them. His *ijtihād* cannot reach the level of their *ijtihād*. The views of those who oppose them are not to be considered, nor is their *ḥujjah* to be accepted. The reason is that our companions identified the evidences, and distinguished between what was sound and established and what was the opposite of this."

Such statements cause big problems for those who want to legalize picking and choosing from schools. They try to counter them through weak opinions. For example, the above statement of Qāḍī Khān is countered with the following weak view of Ibn al-Qāḍī Samāwah: "This is a matter of belief, otherwise Mālik was ahead of them, and there is no evidence that they gathered and followed *akhbār* and *āthār* more than Shāfi'ī and Mālik. And, the traditions had not been compiled during the time of Abū Ḥanīfah and his companions like they were in the times after them, because the six books were compiled later on." The futility of this argument is obvious. We have argued that the jurists worked for 150 years till the law was recorded by Imām Muḥammad. It took another 100 years for the six sound compilations to appear. If compilation is the standard, then it will cause many problems for all the schools. Does this mean that all the jurists had been working in this area without traditions? Should these schools be swept aside and we should start anew from the date of compilation? These books were compiled more than sixty years after al-Shāfi'ī, so does it mean that he was also not aware of traditions? And, it is interesting to note that Abū 'Ubayd, writing 25 years after al-Shāfi'ī's death, does not even mention him in his *Kitāb al-Amwāl*, but his book is full of the views of the Ḥanafī jurists. In other words, al-Shāfi'ī was not even recognized at that time.

Qāḍī Khān's argument is totally in line with the *qā'idah* laid down by Imām al-Karkhī. The conclusion is that even if by one chance in thousands a jurist, and he has to be a *mujtahid*, discovers that a tradition was not followed by Abū Ḥanīfah, a fact that this jurist must prove, he cannot go beyond the confines of the school. Ibn 'Ābidīn adds to this that if such a jurist is convinced that he is right, he may follow his view in his personal actions, but he cannot issue a *fatwā* on the basis of his view.

6.4.1.3 The Vital Role of Traditions and Modern Issues

In the above paragraphs we have come to recognize the rule that it is very difficult, if not impossible, to question the views of the earlier Imāms on the basis of a sound tradition, which may appear to conflict with their views. In order to question their views on the basis of a tradition, the jurist has to be a *mujtahid muṭlaq* or at least as skilled as a *mujtahid fi'l-madhhab*. It is obvious that such a jurist is not to be found today. Even if such a jurist were to be found, he will not be able to show that the earlier Imāms did not take the tradition into account, because the rule within the school is that the Imāms did take all the traditions into account and they have the juristic experience of 150 years to strengthen this presumption. This rule prevents an established school from being wiped out by persons who do not meet the required qualifications.

Beyond this, the sound compilations have a huge role to play. Without going into too many details, we can easily say that the (new) rules settled by later jurists can be questioned on the basis of sound traditions. In addition to this, the traditions are needed to settle many new issues that did not arise during the period of the earlier or later Imams or have not been addressed by them.

It is important to note that the schools of law did not address all problems. They were more concerned with those issues that arose directly, or by implication, from the texts. Many of these areas were left to the ruler or the Imam to settle. The reason why such rules were left to the rulers was that these were rules that were subject to change over time. The jurists, on the other hand, were concerned more with rules of a permanent nature.[40] We may mention that this is a gigantic area that needs the collective effort of all qualified jurists so that unqualified persons do not try to fill the vacuum. In this effort, the sound compilations of traditions have a huge role to play.

We may now turn to the issue of picking and choosing proper, and to its offshoot called *talfīq*.

---

40. Please examine our book on the subject. Nyazee, *Theories of Islamic Law*,

6.4.2 Picking and Choosing or the Varieties of *Talfīq*

6.4.2.1 The Meaning in General

Picking or choosing opinions or creating a patched up rule essentially means choosing opinions from other schools in preference to the view in one's own school. Picking and choosing may be done in a manner that amounts to choosing a single view, overturning the school view, but without making a patchwork. It may also be done in a manner through which a component of a rule is chosen and is combined with other components of the rule in the school. All this will be clear from the examples provided below. The two processes, and more may be invented, are technically the same from the perspective of methodology. When a number of opinions are chosen from other schools, but they apply to unrelated issues, the process is picking and choosing, which is justified and upheld by many today. When a number of opinions are chosen from different schools and converge in a single issue, the process is called *talfīq*, and is condemned by many, even today, as the pursuit of personal desires and whims or playing with the rules of religion. Different rules and justifications are assigned to the two processes. In our view, at the very basic level the two processes are the same and that is choosing from another school. Justifying picking and choosing will always lead to *talfīq*.

We will first provide a few examples to understand the processes, and then consider some of the views and arguments of those who justify these processes and consider them valid.

Ibn 'Ābidīn says that a person who has performed *wuḍū'* has some blood flowing from his body and he then touches his wife and prays, then the validity of this prayer is based upon *talfīq* that is patched up from the view of the Shāfi'ī and Ḥanafī schools, but such *talfīq* is *bāṭil* so the validity is negated. Mawlānā Ashraf 'Alī Thānawī explains this as follows: When blood oozes out, *wuḍū'* is annulled according to the Ḥanafīs, but not according to the Shāfi'īs. Here the person adopts the Shāfi'ī school. When he touches his wife, his *wuḍū'* is annulled according to the Shāfi'īs, but not according to the Ḥanafīs. Now he adopts the Ḥanafī school. The reality is that his *wuḍū'* stands anulled according to both schools.[41]

Mawlānā Thānawī gives another example: If a person in the state of *wuḍ** touches his wife, submits to cupping, and touches his penis, and then does not perform *wuḍū'* and prays, whichever school he asks will declare his prayer to be a nullity when all three acts are combined. This is called *talfīq*.[42]

We wish to emphasize that the learned Mawlānā Thānawī rejects picking and choosing and *talfīq*, because he maintains that Dīn means obedience and this method means the pursuit of whims. He declares it to be a very dangerous thing, because the person leaves one school for another due to worldly considerations. He then quotes an illustration taken from Ibn 'Ābidīn who says that a jurist proposed to a traditionist for his daughter's hand. The father of the girl said that I will accept on the condition that you perform *raf' yadayn* and proclaim the *āmīn* in an audible voice. The jurist accepted and was married to the girl. This incident was narrated to a learned man, who on hearing it lowered his head (looked down) and said: I fear for his faith (*īmān*) for he adopted the acts for this world and not for some *dalīl shar'ī*.[43]

6.4.2.2 Using the Qāḍī as the Standard

The learned Mawlānā (God bless him), however, did deem the adopting the view of a different school permissible with certain conditions. He stated: If one acts on the view of another school **due to necessity, then one must act on all the constituent parts of this act** (that is, according to what the other school says). This is its condition.

He then adds that "not in rituals, but in *mu'āmalāt* in which there is frequent trial, I (sometimes) issue a *fatwā* according to another Imām when there is a possibility of accommodation, and I do it for removal of hardship. Although I was satisfied about this exemption myself, yet I took permission for this from Mawlānā Rashīd Aḥmad Gangohi (God bless him). I had asked whether a

41. Thānawī, *Ijtihād-o-Taqlīd*, 67.
42. Ibid., 67.
43. Ibid., 68.

fatwā can be issued according to the view of another Imām in cases of necessity. He responded by saying that it is permitted, but this ease is granted only for *mu'āmalāt*."[44]

Now, why did the learned 'Allāmah Gangohi permit the following of another jurist's opinion, and just for the *mu'āmalāt*? The analogy appears to have been borrowed from the rules for the *qāḍī*, who does not decide matters of *'ibādāt*, but focuses on the *mu'āmalāt* alone. It was for this reason that 'Allāmah Gangohi narrowed down the permission to *mu'āmalāt*. But what reasoning was he relying on for permitting the reliance upon another school. The source, in our view, is Imām Abū Bakr al-Kāsānī. He lays down the following rules for the *qāḍī*:

- Where the *qāḍī* is not qualified to undertake *ijtihād*, he is to memorise all the points of agreement and disagreement in the school, otherwise he is to seek a *fatwā*.
- Where the *qāḍī*, who is not a *mujtahid*, decides according to the view of another school, and is aware of this, his judgement is not to be executed.
- Where the *qāḍī*, who is a *mujtahid*, decides according to the view of another school his judgement is valid by consensus.

These points have been extracted from our translation of Imām al-Kāsānī's *Adab al-Qāḍī*. The first two points make it absolutely clear that a *muqallid qāḍī* can under no circumstances change his school and move to the view of another school. The words "and is aware of this" exclude the case of forgetfulness (*nisyān*), which is a defect for one's legal capacity and we need not bother about here. **As the *muftī*'s role is almost the same as that of the *qāḍī*, a *muqallid muftī* can under no circumstances move to the view of another school, otherwise his *fatwā* is of no consequence.** As all *muftīs* today are *muqallids* (relying on the statement of Ibn al-Humām), the matter of picking and choosing should be considered settled just by this rule, that is, picking and choosing from other schools is

44. Thānawī, *Ijtihād-o-Taqlīd*, 68.

prohibited. Nevertheless, some jurists today may consider themselves *mujtahids* of some kind, therefore, we need to consider the third point, which appears to grant permission.

The third point is a classic case where readers forget the underlying rules, or neglect to relate rules, and just read the opinions. The underlying rule of the third point has been laid down by Imām al-Dabbūsī as the second form of permitted *taqlīd*. The rule is that the *taqlīd* by one jurist of another is permitted if the superiority in knowledge of the other is established or acknowledged. This rule permits the Ṣaḥibayn—Imāms Abū Yūsuf and Muḥammad—to undertake *taqlīd* of Abū Ḥanīfah (God be pleased with him), whom they acknowledge as their superior in knowledge. Thus, they follow his *uṣūl* by means of which they come to belong to the Ḥanafī school, and they often follow him in *furū'*, which is what the third point is talking about. Let us reproduce what Imām al-Kāsānī has said so that the issue can be understood in its proper perspective.

فأمّا إذا كان من أهل الاجتهاد ينبغي أن يصحّ قضاؤه في الحكم بالإجماع ولا يكون لقاض آخر أن يبطله لأنّه لا يصدّق على النّسيان بل يحمل على أنّه اجتهد فأدّى اجتهاده إلى مذهب خصمه فقضى به فيكون قضاؤه باجتهاده فيصحّ .

After translating this, we followed it up with comments:

Translation: When the *qāḍī* is qualified to undertake *ijtihād*, it is necessary that his judgement be valid for the case, and this is so by consensus (*ijmā'*). Another *qāḍī* does not have the right to annul it, because it does not fall under the case of forgetfulness, but is to be treated as if he has undertaken *ijtihād*, and his *ijtihād* has led him to the view of his rival school, and he ruled accordingly. As he decided according to his *ijtihād*, his view is valid.

Comments: The situation is a little more complex in our view. The jurist acting as a *qāḍī* and using his own *ijtihād* may be of two types. First is a fully independent *mujtahid* (*mujtahid muṭlaq*). Such a jurist does not perform *taqlīd* either in *uṣūl* or in the *furū'*. He has his own set of *uṣūl*. The only condition is that he must declare his *uṣūl* so that other jurists can understand his reasoning, and some may even choose to follow him. This jurist must always follow his own *ijtihād*. He is in no case to follow another school. It is obvious that such a *qāḍī* is not intended here.

The *qāḍī* intended here is one who is called a *mujtahid fī al-madhhab,* like Abū Yūsuf and Muḥammad (God bless them), or a *mujtahid fī al-masā'il,* like Abū Bakr al-Jaṣṣāṣ and al-Sarakhsī (God bless them). These are jurists who perform *taqlīd* with respect to the *uṣūl,* but are more or less independent with respect to the *furū',* that is, while using the *uṣūl* of the school they may arrive at different opinions. If such a *qāḍī* decides according to the opinion of a rival school, the question arises as to what were the *uṣūl* used by him? If such a *qāḍī,* while using the *uṣūl* of his own school arives at the opinion also upheld by a rival school, his opinion is valid, and it is this *qāḍī* who is discussed by Imām al-Kāsānī here. If he does not use the *uṣūl* of his own school and then arrives at the opinion of a rival school, then logically, his opinion is not valid and nor will be his judgement. Modern scholars who are picking and choosing opinions from rival schools today should keep this in mind.

Let us now add to these comments. In the case mentioned by Imām al-Kāsānī, **the *mujtahid* exercised *ijtihād* and by chance his view came to coincide with the view of the Imām of a rival school.** There is absolutely no problem with this, and it is permitted as has been demonstrated by al-Kāsānī. Excercising his own *ijtihād,* according to the *uṣūl* of his school, and picking up a view of the rival school without *ijtihād* are two very different things. In the first case, where the view is based on *ijtihād,* the jurist is not acknowledging the superiority of the Imām of the rival school; in the second case he is. Imām al-Shāfi'ī undertook *ijtihād* himself, and many times his view would conform with the view of Abū Yūsuf, or Muḥammad, or Zufar. Does this mean that he is acknowledging the superiority of these jurists and performing *taqlīd* of these Imāms? Certainly not. As compared to him, al-Shāshī al-Qaffāl, who was not really a *muqallid* although he was an expert in Shāfi'ī *fiqh,* is reported to have said to a questioner: "If you want al-Shāf'ī's view, this is it, but if you want my personal opinion, I will opt for Abū Ḥanīfah's view." His personal opinion here means his own *ijtihād,* which came to coincide with the view of Abū Ḥanīfah.

It does not mean that he became a *muqallid* like Imāms Abū Yūsuf and Muḥammad (God bless them both).

The conclusion we draw from this is that when a *muftī* in the Ḥanafī school chooses Imām al-Shāfi'ī's view, for example, he comes to acknowledge, first, that Imām al-Shāfi'ī is superior to this jurist, which is acceptable, but when he chooses his view over the view of Imām Abū Ḥanīfah or that of the school, he has declared that Imām Shāfi'ī is superior in knowledge to the Imāms of the Ḥanafī school. The same applies when he chooses Imām Mālik's view without *ijtihād*. In short, this jurist has moved out of the Ḥanafī school and has become a *muqallid* of another Imām.

If the jurist is doing so on the basis of his *ijtihād* as explained above, he does not move out of the school. This is what Ibn 'Ābidīn has also indicated on a few occasions. **He definitely moves out of the Ḥanafī school when he merely picks and chooses, and cannot be considered a Ḥanafī.** Further, mere claims of necessity and change of circumstances (*'urf*) are not *ijtihād* in the sense meant here.

6.4.2.3 Rules That Prohibit Picking and Choosing

The debate about picking and choosing opinions from other schools, and about *talfīq*, has been going on for some time. The only way to resolve this issue and to come to a definitive conclusion about the right course of action is to consider certain rules that apparently prohibit this practice. Before we list the rules and explain them, it is important to note that *talfīq*, as practiced or conceived in the example of *wuḍū'* above where pieces of different views are combined for permissibility, is rejected by most jurists and is considered *bāṭil*. The condition imposed by jurists like Mawlānā Thānawī is that the whole issue should be followed according to one school. In other words, if you pick and choose, choose the entire issue making the choosing complete; choosing of pieces is not allowed. The reasoning is that choosing of pieces amounts to an open and uncontrolled pursuit of desires and amounts to playing with the Dīn. Accordingly, when we come to reject picking and choosing, *talfīq* is automatically condemned. We may now list the rules:

1. *Rule 1: Taqlīd* by a *mujtahid* of another *mujtahid* is allowed if the superiority in knowledge of the other *mujtahid* is acknowledged and accepted (al-Dabbūsī).

2. *Rule 2:* The truth is one, and the truth lies with the jurists of the Ḥanafī school (see Qāḍī Khān above).

3. *Rule 3:* It is prohibited to follow an opinion not preferred—*al-marjūḥ ka'l-'adam* (Ibn 'Ābidīn and others).

4. *Rule 4:* It is prohibited to follow a weak (*ḍa'īf*) view (Ibn 'Ābidīn and others).

5. *Rule 5:* Anyone who chooses opinions from rival schools or undertakes *talfīq* is in violation of the *qawānīn uṣūliyyah,* which represent the essence of *taqlīd* and determine the meaning of a school of Islamic law (the position taken in these modules).

Let us take up these rules one by one:

The first rule, that is, "*taqlīd* by a *mujtahid* of another *mujtahid* is allowed if the superiority in knowledge of the other *mujtahid* is acknowledged and accepted (al-Dabbūsī)," has already been discussed above in considerable detail. The conclusion was that by moving to another school, even if it is in one view for whatever reasons, the other Imām is considered superior to our own Imams and *taqlid* of the Ḥanafī school stands demolished.

The second rule, that is, "the truth is one, and the truth lies with the jurists of the Ḥanafī school" is indicated by the statement of Qāḍī Khān above where he says, "The reason, it is obvious, is that the truth lies with our companions and does not go beyond them." The same assertion is made by 'Allāmah Qāsim. At the end of his *Rasm al-Muftī,* Ibn 'Ābidīn first records all kinds of views about this issue in the context of the *qāḍī* or *muftī* preferring the view of another school. He then concludes with a passage from al-'Allāmah Qāsim as follows:

> It is not permitted to the *muqallid qāḍī* to issue a ruling (*ḥukm*) on the basis of a weak opinion. The reason is

> that he does not possess the authority of *tarjīḥ*, therefore, he will only move away from the sound view due to motives that are dubious (unworthy). **If he does issue such a ruling it is not to be implemented, because his judgment is a judgement based on an untruth; because the truth is the sound view.** What is related about the weak view being strengthened by the judgment is intended to apply to the judgment of the *mujtahid*.... What is mentioned in this meaning has been explicitly stated by Ibn al-Humām.

This is the conclusion drawn by Ibn 'Ābidīn. What has been said about the *qāḍī* applies to the *muftī* as well and in much stronger terms, because the *qāḍī* has to give relief to the litigants whereas the *muftī* is under no such pressure.

The rule is actually based on a *qā'idah uṣūliyyah*. The issue is: Is each *mujtahid* right? The majority of the jurists (*jamhūr*), maintain that each *mujtahid* is right. It is in this context that one hears many modern scholars asserting that all four Sunni schools are equally valid representations of the *sharī'ah*, and whichever school is followed is on the right track. The Ḥanafī response to the issue is that each *mujtahid* is not right and the "truth is one," and this truth, according to their belief, lies with the Imāms and jurists of the Ḥanafī school. As Allah alone knows what this single truth is, the Ḥanafī jurists frame the assertion as follows: "If we are asked about our opinions and about the opinions of the rival school, we will say by necessity, 'Our opinions are correct with a probability of our error (in some cases), and the opinions of our rivals are incorrect, with a probability of being correct (in some cases).' " This is stated by al-Ḥaskafī in the opening chapter of his book, and is the general view in the Ḥanafī school. In other words, according to the Ḥanafīs, a person following a rival school has to believe that the truth lies with his school.

For the sake of argument, we may say that if all Sunni schools are correct, why have four schools? Let us have a single school with a huge variety of opinions on every issue in this large school, and let the people follow whatever they like. This will definitely create a mess, and make the implementation of the law impossible.

In the end it will lead to a situation where there are no schools. Perhaps, this is what some groups desire today, so that the rule of the *sharīʿah* comes to an end.

Without going into further details, we may conclude that anyone who chooses an opinion from a rival school is choosing a view that is probably incorrect, and by doing so he is preferring it over a view that is probably, and by belief definitely, correct. By doing so he is violating the fundamental *qawāʿid* of Ḥanafī law.

The third rule is obvious and needs no explanation, that is, "It is prohibited to follow an opinion not preferred—*al-marjūḥ ka'l-ʿadam* (Ibn ʿĀbidīn and others)." The rule simply means that only the preferred opinion within the school is to be followed, and all the other opinions that have not been preferred are to be treated as non-existent. If this is the position about opinions that were based on the *uṣūl* and *qawāʿid* of the Imam, then the view of other schools, based on rejected *qawanīn*, have to be declared as *marjūḥ*. There is no way in which such views can be followed.

Here, we may consider some of the arguments advanced by scholars who uphold the following of other schools with some conditions. The basic condition they impose is that of necessity and need, and also being a matter of widespread use. There is a detailed ruling on the case of cruelty to wives where women were advised to resort to apostasy for seeking release from their cruel husbands when all other avenues of seeking relief were closed in British India. The basis was necessity. The issue was settled by Mawlānā Thānwawī. It is not proper to argue with the learned Mawlānā, for he was a jurist of a very high status, but we find the argument based on necessity somewhat unconvincing. Further, it can lead to the opening of other doors. For example, a man divorces his wife thrice in a state of anger, or by way of jest, or in a state of voluntary intoxication and later realizes the consequences of what has happened; he is terrorized out of his wits due to the prospect of losing his wife and the whole world of the woman collapses around her. Is this necessity enough to move to other schools? The necessity appears to be exactly similar to the one advanced in the case of wives resorting to apostasy. If it is, then many of the rules of the school, so carefully crafted, will stand eroded.

Further, *talfīq* on many occasions may have a similar necessity. Take the example of *wuḍū'* quoted above. It is something that is a matter of general necessity, for every worshipper is affected. As compared to this, the case of wives discussed in the previous paragraph are lesser in terms of generality. Why then is this *talfīq* prohibited, but it is permitted when the need is wider? Further, it is difficult to understand why choosing small parts of opinions from rival schools amounts to playing with religion and choosing a whole opinion does not. These arguments are difficult to digest.

The conclusion is that all opinions of a rival school are to be treated as *marjūḥ*. Where the opinions coincide, the issue is not relevant.

The fourth rule pertains to weak opinions or evidences, that is, "It is prohibited to follow a weak opinion (or *dalīl*)." The jurists are in agreement about this rule. The issue is whether the views of a rival school can be placed in this category. The way the Ḥanafī jurists turn down the arguments of rival schools in their books can easily lead us to the conclusion that as the other school is likely to be wrong most of the time, the views of the other school are weak (*ḍa'īf*), and it is forbidden to follow a view that is *ḍa'īf*.

Here we may take the opportunity to mention that the justification for *talfīq* is derived from the view of Ibn Nujaym, and the view about the permissibility of picking and choosing in general is also strengthened through his views. Ibn 'Ābidīn has partly rejected Ibn Nujaym's work, especially his *al-Ashbāh wa-al-Naẓā'ir*, on the grounds that it relies on the views of rival schools on many occasions. It is true that Ibn Nujaym copies copiously from other schools, especially the Shāfi'ī school. It is for the same reason that Ibn 'Ābidīn counters him on many occasions. We have recorded a few in this document, especially the view about following the view of the Imām alone. The point is that even if the work of Ibn Nujaym is deemed reliable, his opinion cannot serve as a basis for justifying *talfīq* as compared to all the rules and views that have been quoted above. An interesting point, however, is to be noted that Ibn Nujaym approves the following of the views of other schools and also approves *talfīq*, but then contradicts himself on the issue of changing schools. Thus, he says that if a person leaves our school and goes to the Shāfi'ī school, but then comes back, we will give him *ta'zīr* for going to a lesser (*adwan*) school. Is he saying that the views of the Shāfi'ī school are to be placed in the category of the *ḍa'īf*? We believe that is what he is saying.

The fifth and the last rule is: "Anyone who chooses opinions from rival schools or undertakes *talfīq* is in violation of the *qawānīn uṣūliyyah*, which represent the essence of *taqlīd* and determine the meaning of a school of Islamic law." This is a rule that has been asserted again and again in all the previous modules and even in this module. We have been arguing throughout these modules that a school is a body or rules of interpretation or its *uṣūl*. These *uṣūl* being an internally consistent set that gives rise to a school stand smashed when movement within schools is not restricted. The following table illustrates what a person who chooses views from different schools at random may be doing in reality. We have chosen only three rules to illustrate the act of a person who is choosing from the Shāfi'ī school.

Principle	**Binding?/ Valid?**	**Not Binding?/ Not Valid?**
Opinion of a Companion	Yes	Yes
Istiḥsān	Yes	Yes
'Āmm is *Qaṭ'ī*	Yes	Yes

There are numerous other conflicts in the rules of intepretation as explained in the previous modules. If this is not the pursuit of *hawā*, then what is? Picking and choosing is, therefore, *bāṭil* and so is *talfīq*, not only for the *muqallid* but also for the *mujtahid* within the school, because there can be no *mujtahid muṭlaq* today. When some texts point out that the *mujtahid* can follow another school, it apples to an absolute *mujtahid* or the *mujtahid muṭlaq*. The reason is that the *mujtahid muṭlaq* has his own principles of interpretation that are different from those of the Ḥanafī school. The truth is that it is binding on this *mujtahid* to follow his own *ijtihād*; he cannot follow the Ḥanafī school for any rule. As for the *mujtahid fi'l-madhhab*, he follows the principles of interpretation of the Ḥanafī school and has the freedom to differ with the Imām on the basis of his own *ijtihād*, but he cannot opt for the view of another school as that would be a grave violation of the principles of interpretation.

6.4.3 Giving up the View of the School on the Basis of 'Urf and the Changes Over Time

6.4.3.1 The Nature of the Change Expected

In the previous section we have examined the situation where the *muftī* attempts to go against the view of the school by bringing in a view from outside the school boundaries. The present section deals with situations where the preferred view of the school is given up in favour of a view that already exists within the school and which is not the preferred view of the school. This process goes against the established *qā'idah* that says: *al-marjūḥ ka'l-adam* (the view not preferred is non-existent). It may also happen that the view adopted does not exist at all within the school, but is brought in to overturn the existing view of the school, even if this is the view of the Imām or his immediate disciples. This is a violation of what we said in the first chapter about the rulings of the first Imāms becoming binding precedents for later jurists. The significance of this rule was that if this process is allowed and begins occurring frequently, the Ḥanafī school as we know it will disappear and with it will disappear the rules of interpretation that are embedded in these decisions. Nevertheless, we mentioned the rulings of Imām al-Ṭaḥāwī who did bring in his own view in preference to those of the earlier Imāms on a few occasions. If the school has to be preserved, a line has to be drawn somewhere and the rulings of the period above the line have to be declared as fixed. Some of the writers have suggested that *taqlīd* became entrenched in the fourth century of the Hijrah. We would suggest that the line be drawn till the end of the fifth century, and all the rulings before this period be declared fixed binding precedents, that is, rulings that cannot be overturned.

6.4.3.2 The Meaning of *'Urf* as the Basis of Change

Having said that, we may note the cases that Ibn 'Ābidīn has identified in which the rule preferred has been set aside and a new pre-existing rule has been preferred or in which an absolutely new rule has been brought in to overturn the view prevailing in the school. Before we look at the actual cases, it is better to identify the methodology recognized by Ibn 'Ābidīn on the basis of which the rules have been amended or changed. Ibn 'Ābidīn has identified the basis as *'urf* or the prevalent practice. *'Urf* is not to be confused with the concept of "age-old custom" prevailing in the English common law, which is deemed to be law by some, so much so that the courts are considered bound to recognize it. In Islamic law *'urf* is considered many different things. For example, if the people have started using a word different from *nikāḥ* to mean *nikāḥ*, then *'urf* considers this customary usage that must be recognized by the law. In other cases, it conveys the concept of *ma'rūf* or what is considered good by the people. It is also considered in terms of the prevalent practice of the people or what they have become used to, whether or not this is an age-old custom. At times, "need of the people" has also been associated with this meaning if not completely absorbed in the meaning of *'urf*. To simplify the concept we may say that *'urf* is used in the sense of *ma'rūf* or what the people have come to consider good practice, whether or not this is ancient practice. There is, however, a very basic condition attached to consideration of such good practice. We may look at the text of two jurists to understand this better. The first statement is from al-Sarakhsī:

> Our Shaykh, the Imām, used to relate from his teacher that he used to render the verdict of permissibility for the sale of *shirb* without the land. He used to add that there is a manifest *'urf* in it in our land, for they used to sell water on one-half. Therefore, on the basis of manifest *'urf* he used to issue the *fatwā* of permissibility. 'Urf, however, is considered where there is no *naṣṣ* (text) opposing it. The proscription about the sale with

> *gharar* is clearly opposed to this *'urf*.[45]

A few important points are to be noted here. First, the desired *'urf* must not oppose a text. Second, this opposition does not have to be opposition to an express statement in the texts, rather it can be a broad general principle that arises out of the texts. The meaning here is that the principle of prohibition of *gharar* in sales is not derived from a single express statement, but from several like sale of birds in the air or fish in water and so on. Third, al-Sarakshī goes against the ruling given by the teacher of his Shaykh and Imām without blinking; where it is a matter of principles no one stands in his way. He then justifies *istiṣnā'* on the basis of *'urf*.

> The conclusion is that what is taken into account here is *'urf*. Each thing in which the people practice *istiṣnā'* is valid.[46]

Al-Marghīnānī says in *al-Hidāyah* that the *fatwā* for permitting *muzāra'ah* is on the view of the Ṣāhḥibayn, because of the need of the people and also due to the practice prevalent among the people. He adds that *qiyās* is given up in the face of accepted practice, just as it was done in the case of *istiṣnā'*. He mentions "need" along with *'urf*, because all good practices can be recognized when there is an underlying need. The *qiyās* he mentions is one arising from a single text which is: "Do not sell what you do not have." The general implication of this rule has already been restricted in cases like *ijārah* making it *ẓannī*.

We do not need to mention more texts to understand the nature of *'urf* and its recognition. Two fundamental points that we have identified are of crucial significance. These are the absence of opposition of a text or of the general principles arising from the texts. The second is that the practice to be recognized must be based on a general need, which is sometimes translated into necessity (*ḍarūrah*) by the jurists. These principles are important,

45. Al-Sarakhsī, *al-Mabsūṭ* (Beirut: Dār al-Kutub al-'Ilmiyyah, n.d.), vol. 14, 161–62.
46. Al-Sarakhsī, *al-Mabsūt*, vol. 15, 101.

especially the one about the general principles arising from the text. Today, many things are being brought up for recognition on the grounds that there is no explicit text prohibiting them; general principles emerging from the texts are being ignored. Take the case of Islamic banking in which certain types of *ribā* is being justified, *murābaḥah* for the purchase orderer and so on. Ponder over this (as Ibn 'Ābidīn always says).

Finally, if the method used for accommodating necessity is based on picking and choosing from other schools, the process will be governed by the same rules as have been applied in the previous section. In fact, some scholars have claimed it was this method that was used, for example, in the case of wages for teaching the Qur'ān.

6.4.3.3 Bringing Order Into the *'Urf* Methodology

Ibn 'Ābidīn has mentioned about twenty-five or more cases as examples of a change in the rule on the basis of *'urf*. In addition to this, he mentions words used by the people that are adopted as technical terms. Some of the rules he mentions are as follows:

1. The first rule he lays down for the *muftī* is that he must be fully aware of the transactions of the people. He maintains that it has been stipulated for the *muftī* that he be a *mujtahid*, but as such a jurist is not to be found today, the *muftī* must be fully aware of the transaction and the legal rule that is to be altered on the basis of *'urf*. He maintains that it is for this reason that it is not enough for the *muftī* to be knowledgeable with respect to bookish knowledge alone; he must be aware of the transactions and practices of the people. He gives the example of Imām Muḥammad who used to visit artisans or craftsmen in the market. Today, this would mean that the *muftī* should not only understand mercantile practice, but also the law that is applied in the country to govern these practices. The reason is that most transactions have been framed in terms of legal rules, and without knowing the law the transactions cannot be fully understood.

2. The next rule is that *'urf* must not oppose the *sharī'ah,* that is, express texts or the implications of the text. He divides *'urf* into the general and the particular. Neither of these can go against the text, but general *'urf* can result in restricting the meaning of the text. He gives the example of *istiṣnā'* that has been mentioned above.

3. If the *'urf* changes again, the rule has to be changed again. Accordingly, the rule will revert to what it was originally if the circumstances change back to what they were in the first place.

A number of examples mentioned by Ibn 'Ābidīn pertain to procedural law, however, some substantive rules are also mentioned. When we analyze the method of *'urf* elaborated by the learned author, we find that in most of the cases it amounts to a reinterpretation of facts that the rule governs. If the facts have altered, the rule needs to be altered. If the language of the jurists has to be used, we will say that it amounts to a reevaluation of the *manāṭ* or a fresh *taḥqīq al-manāṭ*. Let us examine one or two cases to elaborate what we mean.

The rule that wages were not to be charged for imparting instruction in the Qur'ān was changed to the validity of charges for such services rendered. The reason given was that times had changed and there was a danger of the Dīn going waste. Apparently, it means that dedication and commitment of people to their religion had gone down and if wages were not provided no one would be ready to impart the required instruction and this would lead to the giving up of religious values. The question to be raised here is whether this idea or fact did not occur to the earlier Imams. Has the stipulation of wages really improved the situation? Is it possible that if the rule had not changed, it would have led to really dedicated people entering this field rather than those who were more interested in the wages and worldly gains. There is no empirical study that can support a finding either way and it is just a value-judgment. Accordingly, it is our personal opinion that the original rule should not have been changed.

Another example that is mentioned is that of the *muzāra'ah* or tenancy. Imām Abū Ḥanīfah considered it unlawful, while the two disciples deemed it lawful. The applicable rule was based on the opinion of the two disciples. In our book on the Islamic form of partnerships, we tried to assess the real underlying basis for these rules. Our conclusion was that the applicable rule was *al-kharāju bi'ḍ-ḍamān* or entitlment to revenue or earning is based on the corresponding liability for bearing loss. The Imām probably assessed that when land is contributed from one side there is no actual loss or risk of loss. In the absence of such risk, the revenue earned is not lawful. The Ṣaḥibayn probably assessed that there is some kind of loss as the land gives up something during cultivation and does not recover unless it is left uncultivated for some time. Scientists today will agree with them, however, this loss is temporary as the land gains back its power. Another point may be that the feudal system had set in later and its pressures required that *muzāra'ah* be permitted, otherwise a big loss would be caused to the poor tenants. Today, if the feudal system gives way to corporate farming, the rule laid down by the Imām should be reimposed. Allah knows best.

CHAPTER 7

IMPORTANT RULES IN *SHARḤ 'UQUD RASM AL-MUFTĪ*

Ibn 'Ābidīn created a remarkable document on the subject of *fatwās* and *muftīs*. He has gathered so many references in his book that the need to refer to other sources is eliminated. We will, therefore, rely only on this book and try to extract certain rules from it, and present them in a systematic manner to make them useful.

It is to be noted here that most jurists, including Ibn al-Humām, consider the *mutī* as a person who is a *mujtahid*. Although, this *mujtahid muftī* operates within the school, he has the ability to handle all new cases on the basis of *takhrīj* or other comprehensive methodology followed by the Ḥanafī school. In the opinion of these jurists, the present day *muftī* is merely a transmitter of the views of the Imām in a form that can be followed by the questioner. Nevertheless, there are many individuals today, and have been there in every age, who follow some form of methodology for addressing new issues. This process can never come to an end and there have to be individuals who have to rise to meet this urgent need of the populace (See Mawlānā Thānawī). It is for this reason that al-Shāṭibī says that the *ijtihād* known as *taḥqīq al-manāṭ* can never come to an end.

The rules given below, therefore, apply not only to the *muftī* who is a transmitter of the views, while he is in the process of moving to the status of a person who can address new issues, even if he has not reached that state, but also to the person who has acquired that ability. The person who has reached this stage of expertise is not of the same status as the Mashā'ikh, but he is a qualified individual, and though the methodology he employs may not be as comprehensive as that of the Mashā'ikh, it is a methodology that can settle new cases. The rules given below, thus, apply to both types of experts.

7.1 Basic Rules for the *Muftī*

Rule 1: The *muftī* is to first consult the *mutūn mu'tabarah*, and these are: *bidāyat al-mubtadi'*, *mukhtaṣar al-qudūrī*, *al-mukhtār lil-fatwā*, *al-nuqāyah*, *al-wiqāyah*, *kanz al-daqā'iq* and *multaqā al-abhur*. (p.60)

These books contain within them the *Ẓāhir al-Riwāyah* or the *masā'il al-uṣūl*. They also record the preferred view of the school, and it is this preferred view that is the law for the school. The rules that have not been preferred are also mentioned on occasions, but these are not the law. It is incumbent upon the *muftī* to follow the view preferred by the Mashā'ikh in these *mutūn* irrespective of the view being that of the Imām or one or more of his disciples. The opinion not preferred is non-existent for purposes of the *fatwā*—*al-marjūḥ kal-'adam*.

Rule 2: The *muftī* must consult the commentaries (*shurūḥ*) for what is stated in the *mutūn*, and issue the *fatwā* only when he understands the meaning of what he is conveying to the questioner, even if the *muftī* is a mere transmitter of the view contained in the *mutūn*. It is better if the *muftī* mentions the *matn* on which he has relied, in the *fatwā* and also the *sharḥ*. Al-Kāsānī's *Badā'i' al-Ṣanā'i'* is also a *sharḥ* for this purpose. If there is conflict in the *shurūḥ*, the *muftī* is to rely on Imām al-Sarakhsī's commentary called *al-Mabsūṭ*, which is a commentary on the primary *matn* called *al-Kāfī*.

Rule 3: If the rule is not to be found in the *mutūn*, the *muftī* is to consult the *fatāwā* literature of the Mashā'ikh. The highest priority is to be accorded to *Fatāwā Qāḍī Khān*. In case of conflict between the *fatāwā* and the commentaries, the view in the commentaries is to be preferred. Recourse is again to Imām al-Sarakhsī's *al-Mabsūṭ* for resolving a continuing conflict.

Rule 4: The *muftī* must develop expertise in consulting the *mutūn* and the *fatāwā* for recognizing the preferred view of the school, because such a rule may sometimes not be clear where two or more views on an issue are stated. Each text has its own unique way of stating the rules, although the method of doing so is sometimes stated in the texts themselves.

Sharḥ 'Uqūd Rasm al-Muftī gives the rules for assessing the preferred view from the *mutūn, shurūḥ* and *fatāwā*, but no amount of guidance is enough unless the *muftī* gains expertise through experience. This experience is usually attained under the supervision of an expert *muftī*. It is for this reason that Ibn 'Ābidīn maintains that simply reading books, being taught by the most respected teachers, which means getting certificates and degrees in our times, is not enough for being able to give a *fatwā*. Training is needed for issuing *fatwās*, and the reason obviously is coming to know the nature of the texts that yield the preferred view. The rules stated by Ibn 'Ābidīn are many, for example, it is the first view that is the preferred view in *Fatāwā Qāḍī Khān* and in *Multaqā*, while it is usually the last view in *Badā'i'*. The instructions given by him should be studied. It has to be remembered though that this knowledge and expertise is needed when there is more than one view stated.

Rule 5: If no rule is to be found for the question asked in the *mutūn* or the *fatāwā*, then it is a new question. A *muftī* should not attempt to answer the new question if he feels that he does not possess the expertise to settle the matter in the light of the *uṣūl* and *qawā'id* of the school. It is better to say, "I do not know," however, if the *muftī* knows of another *muftī* who can, then he should consult him, even if such a *muftī* lives in a different city.

Rule 6: The new question may be taken up by the *muftī* who feels that he can settle the new issue in the light of the *uṣūl* and *qawā'id* of the school. In case he chooses to do so, he must give detailed legal reasoning for arriving at the rule. This legal reasoning is meant not only for the questioner but also for fellow *muftīs* with equivalent or better skills who may make suggestions for improvement or amendment.

It must be mentioned here that there is a distinction between the *uṣūl* and the *qawā'id* of the school. The *uṣūl* are irrebuttable and are the basis of *taqlīd*. The jurist within the school, whoever he may be, cannot go against the *uṣūl* of the school, because they are the basis of *taqlīd*. The *qawā'id*, on the other hand, are different. These are presumptions that are generally accepted in the school, but an individual jurist may sometimes go against a generally accepted presumption if in his view the facts are to be interpreted differently, or time has passed and a better appreciation of the facts is available. It is for this reason that Ibn 'Ābidīn, quoting Ibn Nujaym, says that it is not permitted to settle rules merely on the basis of the *qawā'id* and *ḍawābiṭ*. In another place he says that the *Ṣāḥibayn* sometimes went against the *qawā'id* of the Imām. He then asserts that this does not take them out of the fold of *taqlīd*. The reason is obvious, there is nothing wrong with interpreting the facts differently when new information is available. We have devoted a whole module to this issue, and the reader may have recourse to it for a better understanding.

7.2 Who are the Mashā'ikh

Rule 7: The *fatwā* issued by the *muftī* is not to be confined exclusively to the *qawl* of the Imām, rather it is to be based on what the Mashā'ikh have preferred as the view of the Ḥanafī school. This has been elaborated in some detail above.

Rule 8: The *fatwā* issued by the *muftī* cannot overturn or go against the ruling issued by the Mashā'ikh with respect to the views of the earlier Imāms. If there is a conflict between the views of the Mashā'ikh, the *muftī* should try to reconcile the views through a recourse to Imām al-Sarakhsī's text if he has the ability for *takhrīj*; if not, he should consult a *muftī* who has such ability.

Rule 9: The jurists of the school may also be viewed as three types: the Imām, his immediate disciples and the Mashā'ikh. The Mashā'ikh are those who fall into grades three to five described by Ibn 'Ābidīn, however, later jurists are wiling to grant a similar status to Ibn al-Humām as well.

Rule 10: The Mashā'ikh were all *mujtahids*, who stayed within the school and practised the methodology of *takhrīj*. Every *muftī* should try to acquire expertise in this methodology.

The Mashā'ikh are *mujtahids* up to the fifth grade, up to Marghinani. We would say that some of those in the sixth grade were also qualified mujtahids. The levels of expertise go on decreasing the farther we move away from the *uṣūl*.

For example, today, despite our expertise in gathering information, we do not have access to all the information that the earlier jurists had. It will be difficult for us to determine directly what is the authentic narration and what is not, and what is the stronger view and what is not. It is for this reason that we have to rely on the Mashā'ikh.

7.3 Additional Rules

Rule 11: It is not permitted to choose opinions from other schools whether existing or extinct. This applies to the *muftī* as well as the layman and all institutions, commercial or other. The jurists within the school must undertake *takhrīj* to solve all new issues. In particular, they should use a revaluation of earlier facts, which has been called *'urf*. A judgment of the *qāḍī* or modern judge based on picking and choosing is not to be recognized as valid. Any law made by the modern state that is based on picking and choosing is not to be granted legal validity by the community of jurists. A jurist indulging in such methods is not to be recognized as a Ḥanafī jurist.

Rule 12: It is not permitted to indulge in *talfīq*. This applies to the layman, *muftī*, courts, institutions and the state.

CHAPTER 8

WHAT NEEDS TO BE DONE

In the chapters that have preceded, we have tried to assess the nature of the discussions that the jurists have recorded in relation to *fatwās* and the schools. There are two important points that we would like to add by way of explanation to complete this document. The two points are crucial from our perspective.

8.1 Training for Dealing With Variation in Facts

It must have become obvious to the reader that the main task of the *muftī* is to ascertain the rule that is approved by the school on an issue. The sources from which the *muftī* has to discover this rule are not too many. The main texts are a limited number of *mutūn*, some commentaries on them and a few acclaimed *fatāwā* texts. There are intricacies involved in searching for the established rule, but these are by no means insurmountable for a good researcher, which the *muftī* must be. In short, the rule can be ascertained by a *muftī* who has received his basic education and has spent some time undertaking active research under the guidance of an expert or through some other training method.

Nevertheless, we see a proliferation of *fatāwā* literature in each age. Just look at the work of the *muftīs* in the Indian Sub-Continent alone in the last one hundred or more years. There are huge collections of *fatāwās* that have been produced by *muftīs* during this period. Some of these collections are spread over many volumes. What is the need of such literature when the basic texts are few and relatively easy to access, as stated above?

The answer to the above question concerns the very core of the *muftī*'s task and function. To all those who deal with this area, or even those who deal with the law, it is quite obvious that identifying the basic rules approved by the school is not enough; something more is needed. This something more concerns the variation in the facts. It will rarely be the case that the *muftī* will be presented with a set of facts to which the rule can be applied mechanically. Each case will be unique and the set of facts contained in the question will appear like a new case. The rule can only be applied to the new set of facts through a process that jurists have identified as *taḥqīq al-manāṭ*. In simple terms, this means ascertaining or verifying how the identified established rule will apply to the new set of facts. This process is not totally mechanical and needs additional skills on the part of the *muftī*.

This problem also explains why modern *muftīs* have been favouring later books like the *Fatāwā Hindiyyah* and *Hāshiyah* by Ibn 'Ābidīn. The reason is that these works and others like them contain more detail. The *muftī* who relies on them does so in the hope that the case he is facing will be found in such books with a ruling. The *muftī* does find many of the usual cases mentioned in these detailed books. The truth, however, is that no book can ever keep up with the endless variety of cases that keep on arising. In fact, it is this endless variety of cases with unique facts that keeps the *muftī* in business.

To meet this need and to reduce his reliance on detailed books, what the *muftī* needs to do is to understand the underlying reasoning and the rationale of the basic rules that are found in the *mutūn*. Once such reasoning and rationale is understood, the *muftī*, whether he is transmitter or *mujtahid*, will be able to handle each unique set of facts on his own. His reliance on the detailed *fatāwā* books will be considerably reduced as his expertise in legal reasoning increases.

To acquire mastery in such reasoning, the *muftī* must constantly consult works like those by al-Sarakshī, al-Kāsānī and al-Marghīnānī as well as others. Total reliance on detailed *fatāwā* works has taken the *muftīs* away from the works of the great masters. The *muftī*, if he has to be a real *muftī*, must turn back to these great masters.

8.2 Methodology for Areas Not Covered by the School

Jurists of the Ḥanafī school, or those of any other school, did not lay down the complete law. Indeed, they could not have done so because new situations and cases arise in every new age. It is impossible for jurists of one age to lay down the entire law for all times. In our book, *Theories of Islamic Law*, we explained this situation in detail.

The main idea expressed in that work was that Islamic law has a central core. This core has been laid down by the Qur'ān and the Sunnah. Rules derived from these texts by way extension and the use of rational methods are also part of this core. Some of the situations dealt with by the law derived by the jurists did apply to what may be called new situations, but these were handled adequately by the jurists. In the modern age, many new situations have arisen and some problems that were new for the *fuqahā'* have changed forms. Even in the part that lies at the central core, for example the *'ibāḍāt*, some new situations have arisen

The uncharted area not covered by the *fuqahā'* was handled by the governments of different ages under their *siyāsah* jurisdiction. This role kept on expanding with the passage of time, and today it has expanded to take over many aspects of human life. All these are areas in which states pass legislation or matters that the courts handle. All these new situations require rulings from the *muftīs*. The present day *muftī* has confined himself to the *ibādāt* and issues of family law. He must come out of his shell and start handling all these matters, otherwise people without the necessary qualfications will take over matters in the name of Islam; the vacuum created by the *muftī* is bound to be filled by someone.

There is a very important question that needs to be answered. The question is that if the *fuqahā'* did not address certain issues and left them for the ruler, and there are other issues that have arisen after their time, then how are their books or rulings relevant for this task? The answer to this question is that what we need to retrieve from these books are the general principles and propositions recorded by these jurists. It is only these general principles that will ensure that the law to be developed will be in conformity with the norms of the *sharī'ah*. The first task of the modern jurist then is to start cataloguing and elaborating the essential principles of Islamic law. The jurists have left a treasure of such principles for us, along with the *maqāṣid al-sharī'ah* as ultimate priniples. The figure below is expected to elaborate the methodology for deriving these principles and for issuing new rulings.

To handle all these new situations, and this gigantic task, the *muftī* needs a methodology. In the previous modules we have tried to identify this methodology in some detail. The methodology needs to be adopted, refined and developed further if the modern *muftī* has to justify his purpose.

In addition to the above, it is necessary for the *muftī*, when rendering a *fatwā* on a new issue, to give his detailed reasoning. This detailed reasoning may take the form of stating the facts, identifying the issues, stating the governing rule or rules, and analysis of the rules in relation to the facts, followed by the statement of the *fatwā*.

THE METHODOLOGY FOR FATWAS
Imran Ahsan Khan Nyazee

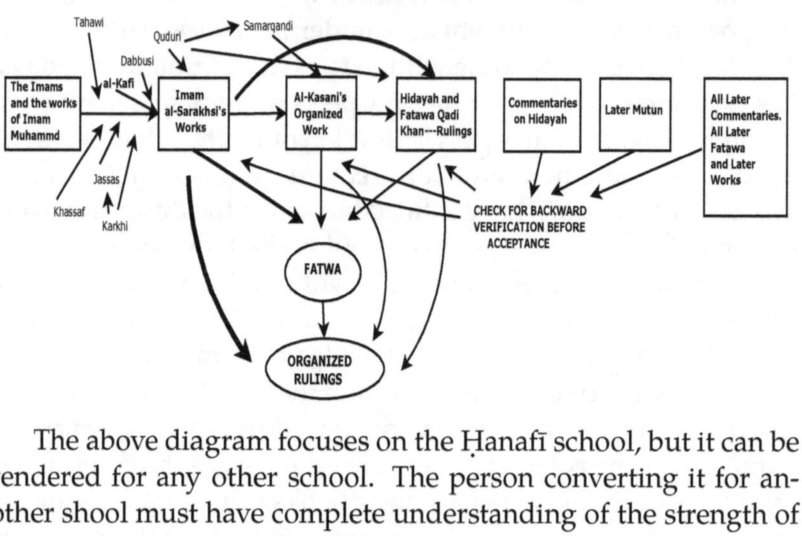

The above diagram focuses on the Ḥanafī school, but it can be rendered for any other school. The person converting it for another shool must have complete understanding of the strength of the various sources in that schools.

BIBLIOGRAPHY

Dabbūsī, 'Umar ibn 'Īsā. *Kitāb Ta'sīs al-Naẓar*. Cairo: Maktabat al-Khānjī, 1994.

Ḥaṣkafī, Muḥammad ibn 'Alī. *al-Durr al-Mukhtār Sharḥ Tanwīr al-Abṣār*. Beirut: Dār al-Kutub al-'Ilmiyyah, 2002.

Ibn 'Ābidīn, Muḥammad Amīn. *Radd al-Muḥtār 'alā al-Durr al-Mukhtār Sharḥ Tanwīr al-Abṣār*. 12 vols. Riyadh: Dār 'Ālam al-Kutub, 2003.

———. *Sharḥ 'Uqūd Rasm al-Muftī*. Karachi: Maktabat al-Bushrā, 2009.

Karkhī, 'Abd Allāh ibn al-Ḥusayn. *Risālah fī al-Uṣūl*. Cairo: al-Maṭba'ah al-Adabīyah, 1902.

Kāsānī, Abū Bakr. *Kitāb Adab al-Qāḍī*. Vol. 5 of *Badā'i' al-Ṣanā'i' fī Tartīb al-Sharā'i'*, edited by Muḥammad 'Adnān ibn Yāsīn Darwīsh, 438–461. Beirut: Dār Iḥyā' al-Turāth al-'Arabī, 2000.

Marghīnānī, Burhan al-Dīn Abū Bakr. *al-Hidāyah: The Guidance*. Translated by Imran Ahsan Nyazee. 4 vols. Bristol: Amal Press, 2006.

Nyazee, Imran Ahsan Khan. *Islamic Jurisprudence*. Islamabad: Federal Law House, 2013.

———. *Theories of Islamic Law: The Methodology of Ijtihād*. Islamabad: Federal Law House, 2007.

Thānawī, Ashraf 'Alī. *Ijtihād-o-Taqlīd kā Ākhirī Fayslah*. Karachi: Zamzam Publishers, 2004.

Appendices

APPENDIX A

ḤANAFĪ SOURCES: *UṢŪL AL-FIQH*

Abū Ḥanīfah, al-Nu'mān ibn Thābit ibn Zūṭā (d. 150/767). *Al-Fiqh al-Akbar*. Cairo, 1323. [Also Cairo: Dār al-Kutub al-'Arabīyah al-Kubrā, 1327/1909. Also Beirut: Dār al-Kutub al-'Ilmīyah, 1979.]

أبو حنيفة، النعمان بن ثابت بن زوطى (المتوفى ١٥٠/٧٦٧). الفقه الأكبر. القاهرة، ١٣٢٣

Māturīdī, Muḥammad ibn Muḥammad, al- (d. 333/944). *Sharḥ al-Fiqh al-Akbar*. Ṣaydā: Manshūrāt al-Maktabah al-'Aṣrīyah, n.d.

الماتريدى، محمد بن محمد (المتوفى ٣٣٣/٩٤٤). شرح الفقه الأكبر. صيدا: منشورات المكتبة العصرية، ـــ

Karkhī, 'Abd Allāh ibn al-Ḥusayn, al- (d. 340/951). *Risālah fī al-Uṣūl*. On pp. 78–87 following al-Dabūsī (d. 430/1039). *Ta'sīs al-Naẓar*. Cairo, n.d. [Also *al-Uṣūl allatī 'alayhā Madār Furū' al-Ḥanafīyah*. Comments by al-Nasafī, Abū Ḥafṣ. Cairo: al-Maṭba'ah al-Adabīyah, n.d.] Urdu translation *Uṣūl-i Karkhī*. Karachi: Islamic Resarch Institute, n.d.

الكرخى، عبد الله بن الحسين (المتوفى ٣٤٠/٩٥١). رسالة فى الأصول. مع تأسيس النظر. القاهرة، ـــ

_________. *Al-Aqwāl al-Uṣūlīyah*. 1st ed. Saudi Arabia: al-Jubūrī, 1989.

_________. الأقوال الأصولية. السعودية: الجبورى، ١٩٨٩

Shāshī al-Samarqandī, Abū Ya'qūb Isḥāq ibn Ibrāhīm, al- (d. 342/953). *Kitāb al-Uṣūl*. Delhi, 1264, 1310. [Also Allāhābād, 1289. Also Luckhnow, 1278, 1293, 1297, & 1337.]

الشاشى السمرقندى، أبو يعقوب اسحاق بن إبراهيم (المتوفى ٣٤٢/٩٥٣). كتاب الأصول. دهلى، ١٢٦٤ ، ١٣١٠

Jaṣṣāṣ al-Rāzī, Abū Bakr Aḥmad ibn 'Alī, al- (d. 370/982). *Uṣūl al-Fiqh al-Musammā bi-al-Fuṣūl fī al-Uṣūl*. Kuwayt: Wizārat al-Awqāf wa-al-Shu'ūn al-Islāmīyah, 1988. [Also *Fuṣūl fī al-Uṣūl*. 1st. ed. Lahore: Maktabah al-'Ilmīyah, 1981. (Excerpts from the author's book).]

الجصاص الرازى، أبو بكر أحمد بن على (المتوفى ٩٨٢/٣٧٠). أصول الفقه المسمى بالفصول فى الأصول. كويت: وزارة الأوقاف والشئون الإسلامية، ١٩٨٨

Dabūsī, Abū Zayd 'Ubayd Allāh ibn 'Umar 'Īsā, al- (d. 430/1039). *Ta'sīs al-Naẓar*. 1st. ed. Cairo: al-Maṭba'ah al-Adabīyah, 1320.

الدبوسى، ابو زيد عبيد الله بن عمر عيسى (المتوفى ١٠٣٩/٤٣٠). تأسيس النظر. القاهرة: المطبعة الأدبية، ١٣٢٠

________. *Taqwīm al-Adillah fī Uṣūl al-Fiqh*. 1st. ed. Beirut: Dār al-Kutum al-'Ilmīyah, 1421.

________. تقويم الادلّة في أصول الفقه. بيروت: دار الكتب العلميّة، ١٤٢١

Sarakhsī, Shams al-A'immah Abū Bakr Muḥammad ibn Abī Sahl Aḥmad, al- (d. 490/1097). *Kitāb al-Uṣūl*. Title page *Uṣūl al-Sarakhsī*. Ed. Abū al-Wafā' al-Afghānī. 2 vols. Cairo, 1372.

السرخسى، شمس الأئمّة أبو بكر محمد بن أبى سهل أحمد (المتوفى ١٠٨٩/٤٨٢). كتاب الأصول. تحقيق أبو الوفاء الأفغانى. القاهرة، ١٣٧٢

Bazdawī Fakhr al-Islam, 'Alī ibn Muḥammad ibn al-Ḥusayn, al- (d. 482/1089). *Kanz al-Wuṣūl ilā Ma'rifat al-Uṣūl*. On the margin of its commentary by 'Abd al-'Azīz al-Bukārī. *Kashf al-Asrār*. 4 vols. in 2. Cairo: Maktab al-Ṣanā'i', 1307.

البزدوى فخر الإسلام، على بن محمد بن الحسين (المتوفى ١٠٨٩/٤٨٢). كنز الوصول الى معرفة الأصول. مع كشف الأسرار. القاهرة: مكتب الصنائع، ١٣٠٧

Samarqandī, Abū Bakr 'Alā' al-Dīn al-Mansūr Muḥammad ibn Aḥmad, al- (d. 538/1144). *Mīzān al-Uṣūl fī Natā'ij al-'Uqūl*. 1st. ed. Baghdād: Wizārat al-Awqāf wa-al-Shu'ūn al-Dīnīyah, Lajnat Iḥyā' al-Turāth al-'Arabī wa-al-Islāmī, 1987.

السمرقندى، أبو بكر علاء الدين المنصور محمد بن أحمد (المتوفى ١١٤٤/٥٣٨

). ميزان الأصول فى نتاءج العقول. بغداد: وزارة الأوقاف والشئون الدينية، لجنة إحياء التراث العربى والإسلامى، ١٩٨٧

Nasafī, Ḥāfiẓ al-Dīn Abū al-Barakāt 'Abd Allāh ibn Aḥmad ibn Maḥmūd, al- (d. 710/1310) *Matn al-Manār fi Uṣūl al-fiqh* [*Manār al-Anwār*]. Istānbūl, 1314–15.

النسفى، حافظ الدين أبو البركات عبد الله بن أحمد (المتوفى ١١٤٤/٥٣٨). متن المنار فى أصول الفقه. إستانبول، ١٥-١٣١٤

________. *Kashf al-Asrār Sharḥ al-Muṣannaf 'alā al-Manār fī Uṣūl al-Fiqh 'alā Madhhab al-Imām Abī Ḥanīfah*. 1st. ed. Būlāq: al-Maṭba'ah al-Kubrā al-Amīrīyah, 1316.

________. كشف الأسرار شرح المصنّف على المنار فى أصول الفقه على مذهب الإمام أبو حنيفة. بولاق: المطبعة الكبرى الأميرية، ١٣١٦

Bukhārī, 'Abd al-'Azīz, al- (d. 730/1330). *Kashf al-Asrār* (commentary on al-Bazdawī's *Kanz al-Wuṣūl ilā Ma'rifat al-Uṣūl*). 4 vols. in 2. Cairo: Maktabat al-Ṣanā'i', 1307. [Also *Kashf al-Asrār 'an Uṣūl Fakhr al-Islām al-Bazdawī*. New offset edition. Beirut: Dār al-Kitāb al-'Arabī, 1974.]

البخارى، عبد العزيز (المتوفى ١٣٣٠/٧٣٠). كشف الأسرار شرح كنز الوصول الى معرفة الأصول. القاهرة: مكتبة الصنائع، ١٣٠٧

Ṣadr al-Sharī'ah al-Thānī al-Maḥbūbī, 'Ubayd Allāh ibn Mas'ūd (d. 747/1346). *Sharḥ al-Tawḍīḥ 'alā al-Tanqīḥ*. 1st. ed. Cairo: al-Maṭba'ah al-Khayrīyah, 1322-24. [Also *Al-Tanqīḥ* and its commentary *Tawḍīḥ fi Ḥall Jawāmid al-Tanqīḥ*. On the margin of its commentary by the Shāfi'ī scholar al-Taftāzānī. *Al-Talwīḥ fi Kashf Ḥaqā'iq al-Tanqīḥ*. 2 vols. in 1. Cairo, 1377/1957.]

صدر الشريعة الثانى المحبوبى، عبيد الله بن مسعود (المتوفى ١٣٤٦/٧٤٧). شرح التوضيح على التنقيح. القاهرة: المطبعة الخيرية، ٢٤-١٣٢٢

Ibn al-Malak, 'Izz al-Dīn 'Abd al-Laṭīf ibn 'Abd al-'Azīz ibn Amīn Firishtah (d. 797/1395). *Sharh Manār al-Anwār* [*Kashf al-Asrār*]. Istānbūl, 1314–15.

ابن الملك، عزّ الدين عبد اللطيف بن عبد العزيز بن أمين فرشتة (المتوفى ١٣٩٥/٧٩٧). شرح منار الانوار. إستانبول، ١٥-١٣١٤

Ḥalabī, Zayn al-Dīn Abū 'Azzī Ṭāhir ibn al-Ḥasan ibn Ḥabīb, al- (d. 807/1405). *Mukhtaṣar al-Manār*. On pp. 2-26 and 155 in *Majmū' Mutūn Uṣūliyah*. Damascus, n.d.

الحلبي، زين الدين أبو عزّى طاهر بن الحسن بن حبيب (المتوفى ١٤٠٥/٨٠٧). مختصر المنار. مع مجموع متون أصولية. دمشق، ـ

Ibn al-Humām al-Sīwāsī al-Iskandarī, Kamāl al-Dīn Muḥammad ibn Humām al-Dīn 'Abd al-Wāḥid ibn 'Abd al-Ḥamīd (d. 861/1457) [Ibn al-Ḥumām, Muḥammad ibn 'Abd al-Wāḥid]. *Al-Taḥrīr fī Uṣūl al-Fiqh: al-Jāmi' bayn Iṣtalāhay al-Ḥanafīyah wa al-Shāfi'īyah*. Cairo: Muṣtafā al-Bābī al-Ḥalabī, 1351.

إبن الهمام السيواسى الإسكندرى، كمال الدن محمد بن همام الدين عبد الوحيد بن عبد الحميد (المتوفى ١٤٥٧/٨٦١). التحرير فى أصول الفقه: الجامع بين اصتلاحي الحنفية والشافعية. القاهرة: مصطفى البابى الحلبي، ١٣٥١

Mullā Khusraw, Muḥammad ibn Farāmurz ibn 'Alī (d. 885/1480). *Mirqāt al-Wuṣūl ilā 'Ilm al-'Uṣūl*. Cairo, 1320. [Also with its commentary *Mir'āt al-Uṣūl*. Istānbūl, 1273, 1282, 1310, & 1321.]

ملّا خسرو، محمد بن فرامرز على (المتوفى ١٤٨٠/٨٨٥). مرقاة الوصول الى علم الأصول. القاهرة، ١٣٢٠

________. *Mir'āt al-Uṣūl fī Sharḥ Mirqāt al-Wuṣūl*. With al-Izmīrī. *Ḥāshiyat 'alā Mir'āt al-Uṣūl Sharḥ Mirqāt al-Wuṣūl*. 2 vols. Cairo, 1304.

________. مرآة الأصول فى شرح مرقاة الوصول. مع حاشية الإزميرى على مرآة الأصول شرح مرقاة الوصول. القاهرة، ١٣٠٤

Ibn Nujaym, Zayn al-'Ābidīn ibn Ibrāhīm (d. 970/1563). *Fatḥ al-Ghaffār bi Sharh Manār al-Anwār*. 3 vols. in 1. Cairo, 1355.

إبن نجيم، زين العابدين بن إبراهيم (المتوفى ١٥٦٣/٩٧٠). فتح الغفّار بشرح منار الأنوار. القاهرة، ١٣٥٥

________. *Al-Ashbāh wa al-Naẓā'ir*. Cairo, 1387/1968.

________. الأشباه والنظائر. القاهرة، ١٣٨٧/١٩٦٨

Ibn al-Ḥalabī, Riyaḍ al-Dīn Muḥammad ibn Ibrāhīm (d. 971/1564). *Anwār al-Ḥālik 'alā Sharḥ al-Manār*. On the bottom margin in Ibn al-Mālik (797/1395). *Sharḥ Manār al-Anwār*. Istānbūl, 1315.

إبن الحلبي، رياض الدين محمد بن إبراهيم (المتوفى ١٥٦٤/٩٧١). أنوار الحالك على شرح المنار. مع شرح منار الأنوار. إستانبول، ١٣١٥

Amīr Bādshāh, Muḥammad Amīn (d. 987/1579). *Taysīr al-Taḥrīr*. 4 vols. Cairo, 1321.

أمير بادشاه، محمد أمين (المتوفى ١٥٧٩/٩٨٧). تيسير التحرير. القاهرة، ١٣٢١

'Azmī'zādah, Musṭafā ibn Muḥammad (d. 1040/1630). *Ḥāshiyah 'alā Sharḥ al-Manār*. On the top margin in Ibn al-Malak (d. 797/1395). *Sharḥ Manār al-Anwār*. Istānbūl, 1314–15.

عزمي زاده، مصطفى بن محمد (المتوفى ١٦٣٠/١٠٤٠). حاشية على شرح المنار. مع شرح منار الأنوار. إستانبول، ١٥-١٣١٤

Ḥaṣkafī, 'Alā' al-Dīn ibn Aḥmad ibn Muḥammad, al- (d. 1088/ 1677). *Ifāḍat al-Anwār*. Istānbūl, 1883 & 1300.

الحصكفى، علاء الدين بن أحمد بن محمد (المتوفى ١٦٧٧/١٠٨٨). إفاضة الانوار. إستانبول، ١٨٨٣ و ١٣٠٠

Kawākibī, Muḥammad ibn al-Ḥasan, al- (d. 1096/1685). *Manẓūmat al-Kawākibī fī Uṣūl Fiqh al-Sādah al-Ḥanafīyah*. Al-Ṭab'ah 1. Cairo: Zāhid wa-al-Khānjī, 1317/1899.

الكواكبي، محمد بن الحسن (المتوفى ١٦٨٥/١٠٩٦). منظومات الكواكبي في أصول فقه السادة الحنفية. القاهرة: زاهد والخانجى، ١٣١٧/١٨٩٩

Ḥāmid ibn Muṣṭafā Effendī Qāḍī al-'Askar al-'Uthmānīyah (d. 1098/1687). *Ḥāshiyah 'alā Mir'āt al-Uṣūl*. 2 vols. Cairo, 1280.

حامد بن مصطفى أفندى قاضى العسكر العثمانية (المتوفى ١٦٨٧/١٠٩٨). حاشية على مرآة الأصول. القاهرة، ١٣١٧/١٨٩٩

Izmīrī, Sulaymān ibn 'Abd Allāh, al- (d. 1102/1691). *Ḥāshiyat 'alā Mir'āt al-Uṣūl Sharḥ Mirqāt al-Wuṣūl*. 2 vols. Cairo, 1304.

الإزميرى، سليمان بن عبد الله (المتوفى ١٦٩١/١١٠٢). حاشية على مرآة الأصول شرح مرقاة الوصول. القاهرة، ١٣٠٤

Bihārī, Muḥibb Allāh ibn 'Abd al-Shukūr (d. 1119/1707). *Musallam al-Thubūt*. Hyderabad: Maṭba'at al-'Ulūm, 1297. [Also Kafr al-Ṭammā'in: al-Maṭba'ah al-Ḥusaynīyah al-Miṣrīyah, 1326.]

بهارى، محبّ الله بن عبد الشكور (المتوفى ١١١٩/١٧٠٧). مسلّم الثبوت. حيدرآباد: مطبعة العلوم، ١٢٩٧

Mullā Jīwan, Aḥmad ibn Abī Sa'īd [Shaykh Mullā] (d. 1129/1717). *Nūr al-Anwār ma' Ḥāshiyah Qamar al-Aqmār*. Dehli: Kutub'khānah Rashīdīyah, 1946.

ملّا جيون، أحمد بن أبى سعيد (المتوفى ١١٢٩/١٧١٧). نور الأنوار مع حاشية قمر الأقمار. دهلى: كتب خانه رشيدية، ١٩٤٦

Nābulusī, 'Abd al-Ghanī ibn Ismā'īl, al- (d. 1144/1731). *Khulāṣat al-Taḥqīq fī Bayān Ḥukm al-Taqlīd wa-al-Talfīq: [Al-Juz' al-Awwal min Kitāb al-Ḥadīqah al-Nadīyah Sharḥ al-Ṭarīqah al-Muḥammadīyah]*. Istānbūl: al-Maktabah 'Ishīq, 1978.

النابلسى، عبد الغنى بن إسماعيل (المتوفى ١١٤٤/١٧٣١). خلاصة التحقيق فى بيان حكم التقليد والتلفيق. إستانبول: المكتبة عشيق، ١٩٧٨

Bahr al-'Ulūm, Muḥammad 'Abd al-'Alī ibn Niẓām al-Dīn Muḥammad al-Anṣārī al-Lakhnawī (d. 1180/1766). *Fawātiḥ al-Raḥamūt Sharḥ Musallam al-Thubūt*. Būlāq, 1322. [Also Reprinted Baghdād, 1970.]

بحر العلوم، محمد عبد العلى بن نظام الدين محمد الأنصارى اللكهنوى (المتوفى ١١٨٠/١٧٦٦). فواتح الرحموت شرح مسلّم الثبوت. بولاق، ١٣٢٢

Ibn 'Ābidīn, Muḥammad Amīn ibn 'Umar ibn 'Abd al-'Azīz (d. 1252/1837). *Nasmāt al-Asḥār Ḥāshiyah 'alā Ifāḍat al-Anwār*. Cairo, 1300.

إبن عابدين، محمد أمين بن عمر بن عبد العزيز (المتوفى ١٢٥٢/١٨٣٧). نسمات الأسحار حاشية على إفاضة الأنوار. القاهرة، ١٣٠٠

'Abd al-Ḥalīm al-Lakhnawī, Aḥmad 'Abd al-Ḥalīm ibn Mawlānā Amīn Allāh (d. 1258/1842). *Qamr al-Aqmār 'alā Nūr al-Anwār*. Alongwith Mullā Jīwan. *Nūr al-Anwār*. Cairo, 1316 & Delhi, 1946.

عبد الحليم اللكهنوى، أحمد عبد الحليم بن مولانا أمين الله (المتوفى ١٢٥٨/١٨٤٢). قمر الأقمار على نور الأنوار. مع نور الأنوار. القاهرة، ١٣١٦ ودهلى، ١٩٤٦

Ṣafī al-Hindī, Muḥammad ibn 'Abd al-Raḥīm (d. 1315/1897).

al-Fā'iq fī Uṣūl al-Fiqh. Cairo: Dār al-Ittiḥād al-Akhawī lil-Ṭibā'ah, 1411.

صفى الهندى، محمد بن عبد الرحيم (المتوفى ١٣١٥/١٨٩٧). الفائق فى أصول الفقه. القاهرة: دار الاتّحاد الأخوى للطبعة، ١٤١١

Maḥallāwī al-Ḥanafī, Muḥammad ibn 'Abd al-Raḥmān, al-. *Taḥsīl al-Wuṣūl ilā 'Ilm al-Uṣūl.* Cairo, 1341.

المحلاوى الحنفى، محمد بن عبد الرحمان. تحصيل الوصول إلى علم الأصول. القاهرة، ١٣٤١

Ruhāwī, Abū Zakariyā Yaḥyā, al-. *Ḥāshiyah 'alā Sharḥ al-Manār.* At bottom center of page in Ibn al-Malak (d. 797/1395). *Sharḥ al-Manār.* 1315.

الرهاوى، ابو زكريا يحيي. حاشية على شرح المنار. مع شرح المنار. ١٣١٥

APPENDIX B

ḤANAFĪ SOURCES: *FIQH*

Abū Yūsuf Ya'qūb ibn Ibrāhīm ibn Ḥabīb al-Kūfī al-Anṣārī (d. 182/798). *Kitāb al-Āthār* (*Musnad* of Abū Ḥanifa with added reports). Beirut, 1355. [Also *Kitāb al-Āthār*. Beirut: Dār al-Kutub al-'Ilmīyah, 1978.]

أبو يوسف يعقوب إبراهيم بن حبيب الكوفى الأنصارى (المتوفى ١٨٢/٧٩٨).
كتاب الآثار، بيروت، ١٣٥٥

_________. *Kitāb al-Kharāj*. Cairo, n.d. Translated by E. Fagnan. *Abou Yousof Ya'koub: Le Livre de l'Import Foncier (Kitāb al-Kharādj)*. Paris, 1921. Also translated by Abid Ahmad Ali. *Kitāb-ul-Kharaj (Islamic Revenue Code)*. Lahore, 1979. Also translated by A. Ben Shemesh. *Taxation in Islam*. vol. ii. *Qudāma ibn Ja'far's Kitāb al-Kharāj. Part Seven and Excerpts from Abū Yūsuf's Kitāb al-Kharāj*. Leiden/London, 1965; vol iii, *Abū Yūsuf's Kitāb al-Kharāj*. Leiden/London, 1969.

_________. كتاب الخراج. باريس، ١٩٢١

_________. *Ikhtilāf Abī Ḥanīfah wa-Ibn Abī Laylā*. Cairo, 1938 [Also Al-Ṭab'ah 1. Cairo: Dār al-Hidāyah, 1985.]

_________. إختلاف أبى حنيفة و إبن أبى ليلى. القاهرة، ١٩٣٨

_________. *Al-Radd 'alā Siyar al-Awzā'ī*. 1938.

_________. الردّ على سير الأوزاعى. القاهرة، ١٩٣٨

Shaybānī, Muḥammad ibn al-Ḥasan, al- (d. 189/805). *Kitāb al-Aṣl*. Ed. Abū al-Wafā' al-Afghānī. 4 vols. (Complete book has not been published). Cairo: Maṭba'at Jāmi'at al-Qāhirah, 1954. [Also al-Ṭab'ah 1. Hyderabad: Maṭba'at Majlis Dā'irat al-Ma'ārif al-'Uthmānīyah, 1966. Also al-Ṭab'ah 1. Beirut: 'Ālam al-Kutub, 1990. Also Karachi: Idārat al-Qur'ān wa-al-'Ulūm al-Islāmīyah, 1986.] Also Ed. Chafik Chehata. *Al-Aṣl: Kitāb al-Buyū' wa al-Salam*. Cairo, 1954. (part of *Kitāb al-Aṣl*).

الشيبانى، محمد بن الحسن (المتوفى ٨٠٥/١٨٩). كتاب الأصل. تحقيق أبو الوفاء الأفغانى. القاهرة: مطبعة جامعة القاهرة، ١٩٥٤

________. *Kitāb al-Siyar al-Kabīr*. Cairo, 1957. Partly translated by Majid Khadduri. *Islamic Law of Nations: Shaybānī's Siyar*. Baltimore, 1966.

________. كتاب السير الكبير. القاهرة، ١٩٥٧

________. *Kitāb al-Ḥujjah 'alā Ahl al-Madīnah*. Hyderabad: Lajnat Iḥyā' al-Ma'ārif al-Nu'mānīyah, 1965. [Also al-Ṭab'ah 3. Beirut: 'Ālam al-Kutub, 1983.]

________. كتاب الحجّة على اهل المدينة. حيدرآباد: لجنة إحياء المعارف النعمانية، ١٩٦٥

________. *Kitāb al-Āthār*. Karachi: al-Majlis al-'Ilmī, 1965.

________. كتاب الآثار. كراتشى: المجلس العلمى، ١٩٦٥

________. *Juz' min al-Amālī*. Al-Ṭab'ah 2. Hyderabad: Maṭba'at Majlis Dā'irat al-Ma'ārif al-'Uthmānīyah, 1986.

________. جزء من الأمالى. حيدرآباد: مطبعة مجلس دائرة المعارف العثمانية، ١٩٨٦

________. *Al-Jāmi' al-Kabīr*. Cairo, 1356. [Also al-Ṭab'ah 2. Beirut: Iḥyā' al-Turāth al-'Arabī, 1979. Also al-Ṭab'ah 1. Lahore: Dār al-Ma'ārif al-Nu'mānīyah, 1981.]

________. الجامع الكبير. بيروت: إحياء التراث العربى، ١٩٧٩

________. *Al-Jāmi' al-Ṣaghīr*. Ed. 'Abd al-Ḥayy al-Lakhnawī. Hyderabad, n.d. [Also al-Ṭab'ah 1. Karachi: Idārat al-Qur'ān wa-al-'Ulūm al-Islāmīyah, 1987.]

________. الجامع الصغير. تحقيق عبد الحيّ اللكهنوى. حيدرآباد، ــ

________. *Kitāb al-Makhārij fī al-Ḥiyal*. Ed. J. Schacht. Leipzig, 1930. [Also *Das Kitāb al-Maḫāriġ fil-Ḥijal des Muḥammad ibn al-Ḥasan aš-Šaibānī*. Hildesheim: G. Olms, 1968.]

________. كتاب المخارج فى الحيل. تحقيق ج. شاخت. ليبزج، ١٩٣٠

________. *Kitāb al-Ziyādāt*. Hyderabad, n.d.

________. كتاب الزيادات. حيدرآباد، ــ

________. *Al-Iktisāb fī al-Rizq al-Mustaṭāb*. Al-Ṭab'ah 1. Dimashq: 'Abd al-Hādī Ḥarṣūnī, 1980. [Also al-Ṭab'ah 1. Beirut: Dar al-Kutub al-'Ilmiyah, 1986.]

________. الاكتساب فى الرزق المستطاب. حيدرآباد، ــ

Khaṣṣāf, Abū Bakr Aḥmad ibn ʻUmar al-Shaybānī, al- (d. 260/874). *Kitāb Aḥkām al-Awqāf*. Cairo, 1322/1904.

الخصّاف، أبو بكر بن عمر الشيبانى (المتوفى ٢٦٠/٨٧٤). كتاب أحكام الأوقاف. القاهرة، ١٣٢٢/١٩٠٤

________. *Kitāb Adab al-Qāḍī*. Cairo: Qism al-Nashr bi-al-Jāmiʻah al-Amrīkīyah, 1978.

________. كتاب أدب القاضى. القاهرة: قسم النشر بالجامعة الأمريكية، ١٩٧٨

________. *Kitāb al-Nafaqāt*. Al-Ṭabʻah 1. Beirut: Dār al-Kitāb al-ʻArabī, 1984.

________. كتاب النفقات. بيروت: دار الكتاب العربى، ١٩٨٤

________. *Das Kitāb al-Hijal wal-Mahāriġ des Abū Bakr Aḥmad ibn ʻUmar ibn Muhair Aš-Šaibānī-al-Haṣṣāf*. "Reprofgrafischer Nachdruck der Ausgabe Hannover 1923." Hildesheim: G. Olms, 1968.

________. كتاب الحيل والمخارج. هلدسهائم: ج. أولمس، ١٩٦٨

Ṭaḥāwī, Abū Jaʻfar Aḥmad ibn Muḥammad ibn Salāmah al-Ḥajrī, al- (d. 321/933). *Al-Mukhtaṣar (fī al-Fiqh)*. Cairo, 1370.

الطحاوى، أبو جعفر أحمد بن محمد بن سلامة الحجرى (المتوفى ٣٢١/٩٣٣). المختصر (فى الفقه). القاهرة، ١٣٧٠

________. *Kitāb Mushkil al-Āthār*. 4 vols. Hyderabad, 1333.

________. كتاب مشكل الآثار. حيدرآباد، ١٣٣٣

________. *Kitāb al-Shurūṭ al-Kabīr*. Baghdād, 1966. [See also Watkin, Jeanne. *Function of Documents in Islamic law*. Albany, 1972. Also *Das Kitāb Aḍkār al-Ḥuqūq war-Ruhūn aus dem al-Ġāmiʻ al-Kabīr fiš-Šurūt des Abū Ġaʻfar Aḥmad ibn Muḥammad Aṭ-Ṭaḥāwī*. Heidelberg: C. Winter, 1927.]

________. كتاب الشروط الكبير. بغداد، ١٩٦٦

________. *Sharḥ Maʻānī al-Āthār*. 4 vols. in 2. Cairo, 1386.

________. شرح معانى الآثار. القاهرة، ١٣٨٦

________. *Ikhtilāf al-Fuqahā'*. Islamabad, 1971.

________. إختلاف الفقهاء. إسلام آباد، ١٩٧١

Abū Ḥanīfah, al-Nuʻmān ibn Muḥammad (d. 363/974). *Iktilāf Uṣūl al-Madhāhib*. Simla: Indian Institute of Advanced Study, 1972.

أبو حنيفة، النعمان بن محمد (المتوفى ٩٧٤/٣٦٣). إختلاف أصول المذاهب. شملا، ١٩٧٢

Jaṣṣāṣ al-Rāzī, Abū Bakr Aḥmad ibn 'Alī, al- (d. 370/981). *Aḥkām al-Qur'ān*. 2 vols. Istānbūl: Maṭba'at al-Awkāf al-Islāmīyah, 1355/1916.

الجصّاص الرازى، أبو بكر أحمد بن على (المتوفى ٩٨١/٣٧٠). أحكام القرآن. إستانبول: مطبعة الأوقاف الإسلامية، ١٣٥٥/١٩١٦

________. *Sharḥ Kitāb Adab al-Qāḍī*. (Commentary on al-Khaṣṣāf's work above). Ed. Farhat Ziadeh. Cairo, 1978.

________. شرح كتاب أدب القاضى. تحقيق فرحت زياده. القاهرة، ١٩٧٨

Samarqandī, Abū al-Layth Naṣr ibn Muḥammad ibn Aḥmad ibn Ibrāhīm, al- (d. 373/983). *Fatāwa al-Nawāzil*. Hyderabad, 1335.

السمرقندى، أبو الليث نصر بن محمد بن أحمد بن إبراهيم (المتوفى ٩٨٣/٣٧٣). فتاوى النوازل. حيدرآباد، ١٣٣٥

________. *Khizānat al-Fiqh wa 'Uyūn al-Masā'il*. 2 vols. Baghdad, 1385/1965.

________. خزانة الفقه وعيون المسائل. بغداد، ١٣٨٥/١٩٦٥

Qudūrī al-Baghdādī, Abū al-Ḥusayn Aḥmad ibn Muḥammad, al- (d. 428/1037). *Matn: al-Mu'āmalāt*. Cairo, n.d.

القدورى البغدادى، أبو الحسين أحمد بن محمد (المتوفى ١٠٣٧/٤٢٨). متن: المعاملات. القاهرة، ـــ

________. *Kitāb al-Mukhtaṣar*. Cairo: Maṭba'at al-Taraqqī, 1291/1874. [Also *Qudūrī Fārsī*. Luchnow: Munshī Nūl Kishwar, 1914.] Translated in part with Arabic text by G.H.Bosquet & L. Bercher *Le Statut Personnel en Droit Musulman Hanefite*. Paris, 1952.]

________. كتاب المختصر. القاهرة: مطبعة الترقّى، ١٢٩١/١٨٧٤

Dabūsī, Abū Zayd 'Ubayd Allāh ibn 'Umar 'Īsā, al- (d. 430/1039). *Ta'sīs al-Naẓar*. 1st. ed. Cairo: al-Maṭba'ah al-Adabīyah, 1320.

الدبوسى، ابو زيد عبيد الله بن عمر عيسى (المتوفى ١٠٣٩/٤٣٠). تأسيس النظر. القاهرة: المطبعة الأدبية، ١٣٢٠

Sarakhsī, Shams al-A'immah Abū Bakr Muḥammad ibn Abī Sahl Aḥmad, al- (d. 490/1097). *Kitāb al-Mabsūṭ*. Al-Ṭab'ah 1. 30 vols. Cairo: Maṭbaāt al-Sa'ādah, 1324-31/1906-13. [Also 30 vols. Beirut, 1398/1978; Also 30 vols. in 15 (Reduced photo reprint). Karachi: Idārat al-Qur'ān, 1987/1407.]

السرخسى، شمس الأئمّة أبو بكر محمد بن أبي سهل أحمد (المتوفى ٤٨٢/١٠٨٩). كتاب المبسوط. القاهرة: مطبعة السعادة، ١٣٢٤-٣١/١٩٠٦-١٣

________. *Sharḥ Kitāb al-Siyar al-Kabīr*. Commentary with al-Shaybānī. *Kitāb al-Siyar al-Kabīr*. Cairo, 1916 & 1957. [Also Cairo: Maḥad al-Makhṭūṭāt bi-Jāmi'at al-Duwal al-'Arabīyah, 1971-1972.]

________. شرح كتاب السير الكبير. القاهرة، ١٩١٦ و ١٩٥٧

________. *Al-Nukat*. Hyerabad, 1958. [Also Hyderabad: Lajnat Iḥyā' al-Ma'ārif al-Nu'mānīyah, 1967. Also al-Ṭab'ah 1. Beirut: 'Ālam al-Kutub, 1986.]

________. النكت. القاهرة، ١٩١٦ و ١٩٥٧

Nasafī al-Māturīdī, Najm al-Dīn Abū Ḥafṣ 'Umar ibn Muḥammad ibn Aḥmad, al- (d. 537/1142). *Ṭālibat al-Ṭalabah*. Cairo, 1311.

النسفى الماتريدى، نجم الدين أبو حفص عمر بن محمد بن أحمد (المتوفى ٥٣٧/١١٤٢). طالبة الطلبة. القاهرة، ١٣١١

Samarqandī, Abū Bakr 'Alā' al-Dīn al-Mansūr Muḥammad ibn Aḥmad, al- (d. 538/1144). *Kitāb Tuḥfat al-Fuqahā'*. 3 vols. Dimashq, 1377–79/1958–59. [Also Dimashq: Dār al-Fikr, 1964.]

السمرقندى، أبو بكر علاء الدين المنصور محمد بن أحمد (المتوفى ٥٣٨/١١٤٤). كتاب تحفة الفقهاء. دمشق، ١٣٧٧-٧٩/١٩٥٨-٥٩

Kāsānī, Abū Bakr ibn Mas'ūd, al- (d. 587/1191). *Kitāb Badā'i' al-Ṣanā'i' fī Tartīb al-Sharā'i'*. Al-Ṭab'ah 1. Cairo: Sharikat al-Maṭbū'āt al-'Ilmīyah, 1909–1910. [Also Cairo: Zakariyā' 'Alī Yūsuf, 1968; Also 10 vols. Cairo, 1971; Also al-Ṭab'ah 2. Beirut: Dār al-Kitāb al-'Arabī, 1974; Also al-Ṭab'ah 1. Karachi: H. M. Sa'īd Company, 1400/1980.] *Adab al-Qāḍī* (Book LIII) translated by Imran Ahsan Khan Nyazee, *The*

Unprecedented Analytical Arrangement of Islamic Laws. Islamabad: Federal Law House, 2007.

الكاسانى، أبو بكر بن مسعود (المتوفى ٥٨٧/١١٩١). كتاب بدائع الصنائع فى ترتيب الشرائع. القاهرة: شركة المطبوعات العلمية، ١٩١٠-١٩٠٩

Qāḍī Khān, Fakhr al-Dīn al-Ḥasan ibn Manṣūr al-Awzjānī al-Farghānī (d. 592/1196). *Fatāwā Qāḍī Khān*. On the margin of vols. ii–iii of Awrangzeb 'Ālamgīr's Commission. *al-Fatāwā al-'Ālamgīrīyah*. 6 vols. Bulaq, 1310. Translated in part by Mahomed Yusoof Khan. *Fatawa-i-Kazee khan: Relating to Mahomedan Law of Marriage, Dower, Divorce, Legitamacy, and Guardianship of Minors, According to the Soonnees*. Lahore, 1977.

قاضى خان، فخر الدين الحسن بن منصور الأوزجندى الفرغانى (المتوفى ٥٩٢/١١٩٦). فتاوى قاضى خان. مع الفتاوى العالمكيرية. بولاق، ١٣١٠

Marghīnānī al-Rushdānī Burhān al-Dīn, 'Alī ibn Abū Bakr ibn 'Abd al-Jalīl al-Farghānī, al- (d. 593/1197). *Matn Bidāyat al-Mubtadī*. Cairo. 1368/1948.

المرغينانى الرشدانى برهان الدين، على بن أبو بكر بن عبد الجليل الفرغانى (المتوفى ٥٩٣/١١٩٧). متن بداية المبتدى. القاهرة، ١٩٤٨/١٣٦٨

________. *Kitāb al-Hidāyah*. Cairo: Maṭba'at Shaykh Yaḥyā, 1873. [Also Cairo: Maṭba'at Muṣṭafā al-Bābī al-Ḥalabī wa-Awlādih, 1936. [Also 4 vols. in 2. Cairo, 1368/1948; Also Cairo: Muḥammad 'Alī Ṣubayḥ, 1966. Also Cairo: Muṣṭafā al-Bābī al-Ḥalabī, 1975.] Partly translated by Charles Hamilton, from Persian, in 1772. *the Hedaya, or Guide: A Commentary on the Mussulman laws*. 2nd ed. Edited by S. Grady. London, 1870. Also *The Hedaya*. 1st Ed. Karachi: Darul Ishā'at, 1989. First two volumes translated from Arabic by Imran Ahsan Khan Nyazee, *The Guidance*. Bristol: Amal Press, 2006 & 2008.

________. كتاب الهداية. القاهرة: مطبعة شيخ يحيى، ١٨٧٣

Sajawandī, Sirāj al-Dīn Abū Ṭāhir Muḥammad ibn Muḥammad ibn 'Abd al-Rashīd, al- (d. end of 6th century). *Al-Fatāwā al-Sirājīyah*. Cairo, 1243/1827.

السجوندى، سراج الدين أبو طاهر محمد بن محمد بن الرشيد (القرن ٦). الفتاوى السراجية. القاهرة، ١٨٢٧/١٢٤٣

________. *Matn al-Sirājīyah fī 'Ilm al-Farā'iḍ*. Cairo, n.d. Translated by A Rumsey. *Al Sirajiyyah: or The Mahommeden Law of Inheritance* (reprinted from 1792 translation of Sir William Jones). Rev. 2nd ed. Calcutta, 1890. Also translated by S. Jung. *The Muslim Law of Inheritance*. Allahabad, 1934.

________. متن السراجية فى علم الفرائض. القاهرة، ـــ

Ustarūshanī, Muḥammad ibn Maḥmūd, al- (d. 631/1234) *Jāmi' Aḥkām al-Ṣighār*. Al-Ṭab'ah 1. Baghdād, 1982-83. [Also on the margin of vol. 2 at p.80 in Qāḍī Samāwah (d. 819/1416). *Jāmi' al-Fuṣūlayn*. 2 vols. Cairo, 1300.]

الأستروشانى، محمد بن محمود (المتوفى ٥٩٣/١١٩٧). جامع أحكام الصغار. بغداد، ٨٣-١٩٨٢

Mawṣilī al-Buldajī, Abū al-Faḍl Majd al-Dīn 'Abd Allāh ibn Maḥmūd ibn Mawdūd, al- (d. 683/1284) *Al-Mukhtār* in *Al-Ikhtiyār li-Ta'līl al-Mukhtār*. 5 vols. Cairo, 1386/1966.

الموصلى البلدجى، أبو الفضل مجد الدين عبد الله بن محمود بن مودود (المتوفى ٦٨٣/١٢٨٤). المختار. مع الإختيار لتعليل المختار. القاهرة، ١٩٦٦/١٣٨٦

________. *Al-Ikhtiyār li-Ta'līl al-Mukhtār*. Cairo, 1950. [Also 5 vols. Cairo, 1386/1966.]

________. الإختيار لتعليل المختار. القاهرة، ١٩٥٠

Nasafī, Ḥāfiẓ al-Dīn Abū al-Barakāt 'Abd Allāh ibn Aḥmad ibn Maḥmūd, al- (d. 710/1310) *Kanz al-Daqā'iq fī al-Furū'*. Cairo, 1328. [Also on the margin of Ibn Nujaym (970/1563). *Al-Bahr al-Rā'iq: Sharḥ Kanz al-Daqā'iq*. 8 vols. Cairo, 1333. Also reprint Beirut, n.d.]

النسفى، حافظ الدين أبو البركات عبد الله بن أحمد بن محمود (المتوفى ٧١٠/١٣١٠). كنز الدقائق فى الفروع. القاهرة، ١٣٢٨

Zayla'ī, Fakhr al-Dīn 'Uthmān ibn 'Alī ibn Mihjān al-Barī'ī, al- (d. 743/1342). *Tabyīn al-Ḥaqā'iq: Sharḥ Kanz al-Daqā'iq*. 6 vols. Al-Ṭab'ah 1. Būlāq : al-Maṭba'ah al-Kubrā al-Amīrīyah, 1313–1315. Also reprint Beirut, n.d.]

الزيلعى، فخر الدين عثمان بن على بن مهجان البريعى (المتوفى ١٣٤٢/٧٤٣). تبيين الحقائق شرح كنز الدقائق. القاهرة، ١٣٢٨

Ṣadr al-Sharīʿah al-Thānī al-Maḥbūbī, ʿUbayd Allāh ibn Masʿūd (d. 747/1346). *Sharḥ Wiqāyat al-Riwāyah fī Masāʾil al-Hidāyah* (latter by Ṣadr al-Sharīʿah al-Awwal Burhān al-Dīn ʿUbayd Allāh ibn Maḥmūd ibn Muḥammad al-Maḥbūbī (grandfather of former and brother of al-Marghinānī)). On the margin of ʿAbd al-Ḥakīm al-Afghānī. *Kashf al-Ḥaqāʾiq: Sharḥ Kanz al-Daqāʾiq*. 2 vols. in 1. Cairo, 1318. [Also Quetta, 1986.]

صدر الشريعة الثانى المحبوبى، عبيد الله بن مسعود المحبوبى البخارى الحنفى (المتوفى ١٣٤٦/٧٤٧). شرح وقاية الرواية فى مسائل الهداية. مع كشف الحقائق شرح كنز الدقائق. القاهرة، ١٣١٨

Tarsūsī al-Ḥanafī, Najm al-Dīn Abū Isḥāq Ibrāhīm ibn ʿImād al-Dīn Abū al-Ḥasan ʿAlī ibn Aḥmad ibn ʿAbd al-Ṣamad, al- (d. 758/1356) *Anfaʿ al-Wasāʾil ilā Taḥrīr al-Masāʾil fī al-Furūʿ* or *al-Fatāwā al-Tarsūsīyah*. Cairo, 1344/1926.

الترسوسى الحنفى، نجم الدين أبو إسحاق إبراهيم بن عماد الدين أبو الحسن على بن احمد بن عبد الصمد (المتوفى ١٣٥٦/٧٥٨). أنفع الوسائل إلى تحرير المسائل فى الفروع، أو الفتاوى الترسوسية. القاهرة، ١٣٤٤/١٩٢٦

Bābartī, Akmal al-Dīn Muḥammad ibn Maḥmūd, al- (d. 786/1384) *Sharḥ al-ʿInāyah ʿalā al-Hidāyah*. Commentary on the margin of Ibn al-Humām (d. 861/1457) *Fatḥ al-Qadīr ʿalā al-Hidāyah*. 10 vols. Cairo, 1389/1970.

البابرتى، أكمل الدين محمد بن محمود (المتوفى ١٣٨٤/٧٨٦). شرح العناية على الهداية. مع فتح القدير. القاهرة، ١٣٨٩/١٩٧٠

Ibn ʿAlāʾ, al-ʿĀlim (d. 786/1384). *Al-Fatāwā al-Tātārʾkhānīyah*. Karachi: Idārat al-Qurʾān wa-al-ʿUlūm al-Islāmīyah, 1990.

إبن علاء، العالم (المتوفى ١٣٨٤/٧٨٦). الفتاوى التاتارخانية. كراتشى: إدارة القرآن والعلوم الإسلامية، ١٩٩٠

ʿAbbādī al-Ḥaddād , Abū Bakr ibn ʿAlī, al- (d. 800/1397). *Al-Jawharah al-Nayyirah ʿalā Mukhtaṣar al-Qudūrī*. 2 vols. Isṭānbūl: Maṭbaʿat Maḥmūd Bik, 1301/1884. [Also Cairo, 1322–1323.]

العبّادى الحدّاد، أبو بكر بن على (المتوفى ١٣٩٧/٨٠٠). الجوهرة النيّرة على مختصر القدورى. إستانبول: مطبعة محمود بك، ١٣٠١/١٨٨٤

Mullā Miskīn al-Harawī, Mu'īn al-Dīn Muḥammad ibn Ibrāhīm al-Farāhī (d. *circa* 811/1408). *Sharḥ 'alā Kanz al-Daqā'iq*. Cairo, 1343. [Also *Sharḥ Mu'īn al-Dīn al-Harawī*. Cairo, 1328/1910.]

ملا مسكين الهروى، معين الدين محمد بن إبراهيم الفراهى (المتوفى ١٤٠٨/٨١١). شرح على كنز الدقائق. القاهرة، ١٣٤٣

Ibn Qāḍī Samāwah, Badr al-Dīn Maḥmūd ibn Isrā'īl (d. 819/1416) *Jāmi' al-Fuṣūlayn*. 2 vols. Al-Tab'ah 1. Būlāq: al-Maṭba'ah al-Kubrā al-Amīrīyah, 1300-1301/1882-84. [Also Karachi: Islāmī Kutub'khānah, 1402/1982.]

إبن قاضى سماوة، بدر الدين محمود بن إسرائيل (المتوفى ١٤١٦/٨١٩). جامع الفصولين. بولاق: المطبعة الكبرى الأميرية، ١٣٠٠-١٢٠١/١٨٨٢-٨٤

Bazzāzī al-Kurdurī, Ḥafīẓ al-Dīn Muḥammad ibn Muḥammad, al- (d. 827/1424) *Al-Jāmi' al-Wajīz* or *al-Fatāwā al-Bazzāziyah*. On the margin of vols. i, iv–vi of Awrangzeb 'Ālamgīr's Commission. *al-Fatāwā al-'Ālamgīrīyah*. 6 vols. Būlāq, 1310.

البزّازي الكردرى، حفيظ الدين محمّد بن محمّد (المتوفى ١٤٢٤/٨١٩). الفتاوى البزّازية. مع فتاوى عالمكيرية. بولاق، ١٣١٠

Ṭarābulusī 'Alā' al-Dīn Kawsaj Abū al-Ḥasan al-Ḥanafī, 'Alī ibn Khalīl, al- (d. 844/1440). *Mu'īn al-Ḥukkām fīmā yataraddadu bayn al-Khaṣmayn min al-Aḥkām*. Al-Ṭab'ah 1. Būlāq: al-Maṭba'ah al-Miṣrīyah, 1300/1883 & 1393/1973.

الطرابلسى علاء الدين كوسج أبو الحسن الحنفى، على بن خليل (المتوفى ١٤٤٠/٨٤٤). معين الحكّام فيما يتردد بين الخصمين من الأحكام. بولاق: المطبعة المصرية، ١٣٠٠/١٨٨٣

'Aynī al-'Ayntābī al-Ḥanafī, Abū Muḥammad Maḥmūd ibn Aḥmad ibn Mūsā ibn Aḥmad ibn Ḥusayn ibn Ysusf Badr al-Dīn, al- (d. 855/1451). *Ramz al-Ḥaqā'iq: Sharḥ Kanz al-Daqā'iq*. 2 vols. in 1. Būlāq: Dār al-Ṭibā'ah al-'Āmirah, 1285/1868 & 1320.

العينى العينتابى الحنفى، أبو محمد محمود بن أحمد بن موسى بن أحمد بن حسين بدر

الدين (المتوفى ١٤٥١/٨٥٥). رمز الحقائق: شرح كنز الدقائق. بولاق: دار الطباعة العامرة، ١٢٥٨/١٨٦٨

Ibn al-Humām al-Sīwāsī al-Iskandarī, Kamāl al-Dīn Muḥammad ibn Humām al-Dīn ʻAbd al-Wāḥid ibn ʻAbd al-Ḥamīd (d. 861/1457). *Fatḥ al-Qadīr ʻalā al-Hidāyah: Sharḥ Bidāyat al-Mubtadī.* 10 vols. Cairo, 1318/1900. [Also Al-Tabʻah 1. Cairo: Muṣṭafā al-Bābī al-Ḥalabī, 1389/1970. Also Beirut: Dār Ṣādir, 1972. Also *Sharḥ Fatḥ al-Qadīr lil-ʻĀjiz al-Faqir*. Beirut: Dar al-Kutub al-ʻIlmīyah, 1985.]

إبن الهمام السيواسى الإسكندرى، كمال الدين محمد بن همام الدين عبد الوحيد بن عبد الحميد (المتوفى ١٤٥٧/٨٦١). فتح القدير على الهداية: شرح بداية المبتدى. القاهرة، ١٣١٨/١٩٠٠

Mullā Khusraw, Muḥammad ibn Farāmurz ibn ʻAlī (d. 885/1480). *Durar al-Ḥukkām fī Sharḥ Ghurar al-Aḥkām*. 2 vols. Cairo, 1329–30.

ملّا خسرو، محمد بن فرامرز بن على (المتوفى ١٤٨٠/٨٨٥). درر الحكّام فى شرح غرر الأحكام. القاهرة، ١٣٢٩-٣٠

Jamālī, ʻAlāʼ al-Dīn ʻAlī ibn Aḥmad, al- (d. 931/1525). *Adab al-Awṣiyāʼ*. On the margin of Ibn Qāḍī Samāwinah (d. 819/1416). *Jāmiʻ al-Fuṣūlayn*. 2 vols. Cairo, 1300, beginning at p. 81 of vol. 2.

الجمالى، علاء الدين على بن أحمد (المتوفى ١٥٢٥/٩٣١). أدب الأوصياء. مع جامع الفصولين. القاهرة، ١٣٠٠

Saʻd Allāh ʻĪsā Saʻdī Shalabī (d. 945/1538). *Hāshiyah*. Commentary accompanying Ibn al-Humām (d. 861/1457). *Fatḥ al-Qadīr ʻalā al-Hidāyah*. 10 vols. Cairo, 1389/1970.

سعد الله عيسى سعدى شلبى (المتوفى ١٥٣٨/٩٤٥). حاشية. مع فتح القدير على الهداية. القاهرة، ١٣٨٩/١٩٧٠

Shiblī, Shihāb al-Dīn Aḥmad, al- (d. 947/1540). *Hāshiyah ʻalā Tabyīn al-Ḥaqāʼiq*. On the margin of al-Zaylaʻī (d. 743/1342). *Tabyīn al-Ḥaqāʼiq Sharḥ Kanz al-Daqāʼiq*. 6 vols. Būlāq, 1313-1315.

الشبلى، شهاب الدين أحمد (المتوفى ١٥٤٠/٩٤٧). حاشية على تبيين الحقائق شرح كنز الدقائق. بولاق، ١٣١٣-١٥

Kūhistānī, Shams al-Dīn Muḥammad (d. 952/1546). *Jāmi' al-Rumūz alladhī kāna Sharḥan li-Mukhtaṣar al-Wiqāyah*. Istānbūl: Maṭba'at Muḥammad Yaḥyā, 1289/1873. [Also Istānbūl: Muḥarram Efendī, 1300/1883.]

كوهستانى، شمس الدين محمد (المتوفى ١٥٤٦/٩٥٢). جامع الرموز الذى كان شرحا لمختصر الوقاية. إستانبول، مطبعة محمد يحيي، ١٢٨٩/١٨٧٣

Ḥalabī, Burhān al-Dīn Ibrāhīm ibn Muḥammad ibn Ibrāhīm, al- (d. 956/1549). *Matn Multaqā al-Abḥur*. Cairo, n.d. Translated by H. Sauvaire. *Droit Musulman (Rite Hanafite): Le Moultaqa el Abheur Avec Commentaire Abrege du Madjma' el Anheur*. Marseilles, 1882.

الحلبى، برهان الدين إبراهيم بن محمد إبراهيم (المتوفى ١٥٤٩/٩٥٦). متن ملتقى الأبحر. القاهرة، ـــ

Ibn Nujaym, Zayn al-'Ābidīn ibn Ibrāhīm (d. 970/1563). *Al-Ashbāh wa al-Naẓā'ir*. Cairo, 1322/1904 & 1387/1968. [Reprint Beirut, n.d. Reprint Dimashq: Dār al-Fikr, 1986. Also *al-Ashbāh wa-al-Naẓā'ir 'alā Madhhab Abī Ḥanīfah al-Nu'mān*. Beirut: Dār al-Kutub al-'Ilmīyah, 1985. Also Karachi: Idārat al-Qur'ān wa-al-'Ulūm al-Islāmīyah, 1988.]

إبن نجيم، زين العابدين بن إبراهيم (المتوفى ١٥٦٣/٩٧٠). الأشباه والنظائر. القاهرة، ١٣٢٢/١٩٠٤

________. *Al-Baḥr al-Rā'iq Sharḥ Kanz al-Daqā'iq*. 8 vols. Cairo, 1893 & 1333. Reprint Beirut, n.d.

________. البحر الرائق شرح كنز الدقائق. القاهرة، ١٨٩٣

________. *Al-Fatāwā*. In the margin in al-Khd tīb. *Al-Fatāwā al-Ghiyāthīyah*. Būlāq, 1322. [See also next entry.]

________. الفتاوى. مع الفتاوى الغياثية. بولاق، ١٣٢٢

________. *al-Rasā'il (Fatāwā) al-Zaynīyah fī Fiqh al-Ḥanafīyah*. Beirut, 1400/1980. [Also *Rasāīl Ibn Nujaym*. Al-Ṭab'ah 1. Beirut: Dār al-Kutub al-'Ilmīyah, 1980.]

________. الرسائل الزينية فى فقه الحنفية. بيروت، ١٤٠٠/١٩٨٠

Qaḍī'zādah, Shams al-Dīn (d. 988/1580). *Natā'ij al-Afkār fī Kashf al-Rumūz wa-al-Asrār*. Commentary in vols. 8-10 in Ibn al-Humām (d. 861/1457). *Fatḥ al-Qadīr 'alā al-Hidāyah*. 10 vols. Cairo, 1389/1970.

قاضى زاده، شمس الدين (المتوفى ٩٨٨/١٥٨٠). نتائج الأفكار فى كشف الرموز والأسرار. مع فتح القدير على الهداية. القاهرة، ١٣٨٩/١٩٧٠

Timurtāshi al-Ghazzī al-Ḥanafī, Shams al-Dīn, al- (d. 1004/1595). *Tanwīr al-Abṣār wa Jam' al-Biḥār*. Cairo, n.d.

التمرتاشى الغزّى الحنفى، شمس الدين (المتوفى ٩٨٨/١٥٨٠). تنوير الأبصار وجمع البحار. القاهرة، ـــ

Tamīmī al-Dārī, Taqī al-Dīn ibn 'Abd al-Qādir, al- (d. 1010/1601). *Al-Ṭabaqāt al-Sanīyah fī Tarājim al-Ḥanafīyah*. Cairo: al-Majlis al-A'lā lil-Shu'ūn al-Islāmīyah, 1970. [Also al-Ṭab'ah 1. Riyāḍ: Dār al-Rifā'ī, 1983.]

التيمى الدارى، تقى الدين بن عبد القادر (المتوفى ٩٨٨/١٥٨٠). الطبقات السنية فى تراجم الحنفية. القاهرة: المجلس الأعلى للشئون الإسلامية، ١٩٧٠

Qārī al-Harawī, Ālī ibn Sulṭān Muḥammad, al- (d. 1014/1605). *Sharḥ Mullā 'Alī al-Qārī*. Cairo, 1871. [Also *Fatḥ Bāb al-'Ināyah bi-Sharḥ Kitāb al-Nuqāyah*. 1967.]

القارى الهروى، على بن سلطان محمد (المتوفى ١٠١٤/١٦٠٥). شرح ملّا على القارى. القاهرة، ١٨٧١

As'ad Shaykh al-lslām ibn Abū Bakr al-Qaysarānī al-lskandarānī, al- (d. 1057/1647). *'Uddat Arbāb al-Fatwā* (Organized by Abū al-Su'ūd Muḥammad ibn 'Alī Effendi al-Shirwānī (1207/1792)). Būlāq, 1304.

أسعد شيخ الإسلام بن أبو بكر القيسرانى الإسكندرى (المتوفى ١٠٥٧/١٦٤٧). عدّة أرباب الفتاوى. بولاق، ١٣٠٤

Ibn Ḥamzah, 'Abd al-Ḥalīm ibn Pīr Qadam (d. 1650?). *Kashf Rumūz Ghurar al-Aḥkām wa-Tanwīr Durar al-Ḥukkam*. Būlāq: Dār al-Ṭibā'ah al-'Āmirah, 1853.

إبن حمزة، عبد الحليم بن پير قدم (المتوفى ١٠٦٠/١٦٥٠). كشف رموز غرر الأحكام وتنوير درر الحكّام. بولاق: دار الطباعة العامرة، ١٨٥٣

Shurunbulālī al-Ḥanafī, Abū al-lkhlāṣ Ḥasan ibn 'Ammār al-Wafā'ī, al- (d. 1069/1658). *Ghunyat dhawi al-Aḥkām*. In the margin in Mullā Khusraw (d. 885/1480). *Durar al-Ḥukkām fī Sharḥ Ghurar al-Aḥkām*. 2 vols. Cairo, 1329-30.

الشرنبلالى الحنفى، أبو الإخلاص حسن بن عمّار الوفائى (المتوفى ١٠٦٩/١٦٥٨). غنية ذوى الأحكام. مع درر الحكّام فى شرح غرر الأحكام. القاهرة، ١٣٢٩-٣٠

________. *Kitāb Marāqī al-Falāḥ Sharḥ Nūr al-Īḍāḥ*. Cairo: al-Matba'ah al-'Ilmīyah, 1315/1897. [Also Cairo: al-Matba'ah al-'Āmirah, 1321/1903. Also Beirut: Dār al-Ma'rifah, 1947. Also Cairo: al-Maktabah al-Tijārīyah al-Kubrā, 1357/1938. Also Cairo: Muḥammad 'Alī Ṣubayḥ, 1965.]

________. كتاب مراقى الفلاح شرح نور الإيضاح. القاهرة: المطبعة العلمية، ١٣١٥/١٨٩٧

Shaykh'zādāh, 'Abd al-Raḥmān ibn Muḥammad ibn Sulaymān (d. 1078/1667). *Majma' al-Anhur fī Sharḥ Multaqā al-Abḥur*. 2 vols. Al-Āstānah: Ṭubiā fī al-Maṭba'ah al-'Uthmānīyah, 1258/1842, 1305/1888, & 1310/1892.

شيخ زاده، عبد الرحمان بن محمد بن سليمان (المتوفى ١٠٧٨/١٦٦٧). مجمع الأنهر فى شرح ملتقى الأبحر. الآستانة: المطبعة العثمانية، ١٢٥٨/١٨٤٢

Khayr al-Dīn ibn Aḥmad ibn Nūr al-Dīn 'Alī ibn Zayn al-Dīn ibn 'Abd al-Wahhāb al-Ayyūbī al-'Ulaymī al-Fārūqī al-Ramlī (d. 1081/1671). *Al-Fatāwā al-Khayrīyah li-Naf' al-Barīyah*. 2 vols. in 1. Bulaq, 1300. Partly translated by H. Sauvaire. *El Falawa 'l Khayryeh: Les Fetwas de Khayr-ed-Dyn. Livre des Ventes*. Alexandria, 1876.

خير الدين بن احمد بن نور الدين على بن زين الدين عبد الوهّاب الأيّوبى العليمى الفاروقى الرملى (المتوفى ١٠٨١/١٦٧١). الفتاوى الخيرية لنفع البريّة. بولاق، ١٣٠٠

________. *Al-La'ālī al-Durrīyah fī al-Fawā'id al-Khayrīyah*. Below the text in Ibn Qāḍī Samāwinah (d. 819/1416). *Jāmi' al-Fuṣūlayn*. 2 vols. Cairo, 1300.

________. اللآلى الدرّية فى الفوائد الخيرية. مع جامع الفصولين. القاهرة، ١٣٠٠

Ḥaṣkafī, 'Alā' al-Dīn ibn Aḥmad ibn Muḥammad, al- (d. 1088/ 1677). *Al-Durr al-Mukhtār fī Sharḥ Tanwīr al-Abṣār*. 2 vols. in 1. Bombay: al-Maṭba'ah al-Ḥaydarīyah, 1309/1891. [Also Cairo, n.d. Also in the margin in Ṭahtawī

(1231/1816). *Hāshiyah 'alā al-Durr al-Mukhtār*. 4 vols. Būlāq, 1254. Reprint. Beirut, 1395/1975. Also *The Durr-ul-Mukhtar*. Lahore: Law Publishing Co., 1913.]

الحصكفى، علاء الدين بن احمد بن محمد (المتوفى ١٦٧٧/١٠٨٨). الدرّ المختار فى شرح تنوير الأبصار. بمبئ: المطبعة الحيدرية، ١٣٠٩/١٨٩١

________. *Al-Durr al-Muntaqā*. In the margin in Shaykh'zādāh (d. 1078/1667). *Majma' al-Anhur*. 2 vols. Cairo, 1328.

________. الدرّ المنتقى. مع مجمع الأنهر. القاهرة، ١٣٢٨

Kawākibī, Muḥammad ibn al-Ḥasan, al- (d. 1096/1685). *Al-Fawā'id al-Samīyah fī Sharḥ al-Nuẓum al-Musammā bi-al-Farā'iḍ al-Sanīyah fī Furū' al-Fiqh 'alā Madhhab al-Imām Abī Ḥanīfah al-Nu'mān*. Al-Ṭab'ah 1. Bulāq: al-Maṭba'ah al-Kubrā al-Amīrīyah, 1322–24/1904–1906.

الكواكبى، محمد بن حسن (المتوفى ١٦٨٥/١٠٩٦). الفوائد السمية فى شرح النظم المسمّى بالفرائض السنية فى فروع الفقه على مذهب الإمام أبى حنيفة النعمان. بولاق: المطبعة الكبرى الأميرية، ١٩٠٦-١٩٠٤/١٣٢٢-٢٤

Anqirāwī, Muḥammad ibn Ḥusayn, al- (d. 1098/1687). *Fatāwā al-Anqirāwī*. 2 vols. Būlāq, 1281.

الأنقراوى، محمد بن حسين (المتوفى ١٦٨٧/١٠٩٨). فتاوى الأنقراوى. بولاق، ١٢٨١

Qādiri Effendi, 'Abd al-Qādir ibn Ysūf Naqīb'zādah al-Ḥanafī al-Ḥalābī, al- (d. 1107/1695). *Wāqi'āt al-Muftīn* or *A'māl al-Jām' wa-al-Tadwīn bi-Wāqi'āt al-Muftiyīn*. Cairo, 1300.

القادرى أفندى، عبد القادر بن يوسف نقيب زاده الحنفى الحلبى (المتوفى ١٦٩٥/١١٠٧). واقعات المفتين أو أعمال الجمع والتدوين بواقعات المفتين. القاهرة، ١٣٠٠

Commission of al-Sulṭān Muḥyī al-Dīn Awrangzeb 'Ālamgīr (req. 1069-1118/1659-1707). *Al-Fatāwa al-Alamgīrīyah*. 6 vols. Būlāq, 1310. [Also Deoband: Maktabat Fayḍ al-Qur'ān, 1968. Also reprint Beirut: Dār al-Ma'rifah lil-Ṭibā'ah wa-al-Nashr, 1393/ 1973.] Translated in part in Baillie, Neil. *The Moohummudan Law of Sale According to the Huneefeea Code: From the Futawa Alumgeeree, A Digest of the Whole Law, Prepared by Command of the Emperor Aurungzebe Alumgeer*. London, 1850. Also translated in part in Baillie, Neil. *A Digest of Moohummudan Law on the Subjects to Which it is Usually Applied in British Courts of Justice in India.* 2d ed. Vol. 1. London, 1875. Also translated in part in Baillie, Neil. *Mohammadan Laws on Land Tax According to the Moohummudan Law: Translated from the Fatawa Alumgeeree.* Lahore, 1979.

السلطان محيي الدين أورنگزيب عالمگير. الفتاوى (العالمگيرية) العالمكيرية. بولاق، ١٣١٠

Shurunbulālī, Muḥammad ibn Su'ūd, al-. *Fatḥ Allāh al-Mu'īn 'alā Sharḥ al-Kanz li-Muḥammad Mullā Miskīn.* Cairo: Maṭba'at Jam'īyat al-Ma'ārif, 1870.

الشرنبلالى، محمد بن سعود. فتح المعين على شرح الكنز لمحمد ملّا مسكين. القاهرة: مطبعة جمعية المعارف، ١٨٧٠

Khādimī, Abū Sa'īd Muḥammad ibn Muṣṭafā ibn 'Uthmān, al- (d. 1176/1762). *Ḥāshiyah al-Durar 'alā al-Ghurar.* Cairo, 1310.

الخادمى، أبو سعيد محمد بن مصطفى بن عثمان (المتوفى ١١٧٦/١٧٦٢). حاشية الدرر على الغرر. القاهرة، ١٣١٠

Ṭā'ī, Musṭafā ibn Muḥammad, al- (d. 1192/1778). *Tawfīq al-Raḥmān.* In the margin in al-'Aynī (d. 855/1451). *Ramz al-Ḥaqā'iq.* 2 vols. in 1. Cairo, 1320.

الطائى، مصطفى بن محمد (المتوفى ١١٩٢/١٧٧٨). توفيق الرحمان. مع رمز الحقائق. القاهرة، ١٣٢٠

Ṭaḥāwī, Aḥmad ibn Muḥammad, al- (d. 1231/1816). *Ḥāshiyah 'alā al-Durr al-Mukhtār.* Bulaq, 1254. [Also Reprint. 4 vols. Beirut, 1395/1975. Also *Ḥāshiyat al-Ṭaḥṭāwī 'alā al-Durr al-Mukhtār.* Beirut: Dār al-Ma'rifah, 1975.]

الطحاوى، احمد بن محمد (المتوفى ١٢٣١/١٨١٦). حاشية على الدرّ المختار. بولاق، ١٢٥٤

Akhsīkaythī, Muḥammad ibn Muḥammad (d. 1247/1831). *Al-Ḥusāmī.* Deoband: Muḥammad Isḥāq Ṣiddīqī Mālik Kutub'khānah, 19–?

الأخسيكيتهى، محمد بن محمد (المتوفى ١٢٤٧/١٨٣١). الحسامى. ديوبند: محمد إسحاق صدّيقى كتبخانه، ١٩

Ibn 'Ābidīn, Muḥammad Amīn ibn 'Uthmān ibn 'Abd al-'Azīz (d. 1252/1836). *Minḥat al-Khāliq 'alā al-Baḥr al-Rā'iq.* In the margin in Ibn Nujaym (970/1563). *Al-Baḥr al-Rā'iq*. 8 vols. Cairo, 1333.

إبن عابدين، محمد بن عثمان بن عبد العزيز (المتوفى ١٢٥٢/١٨٣٦). منحة الخالق على البحر الرائق. مع البحر الرائق. القاهرة، ١٣٣٣

________. *Radd al-Muḥtār 'alā al-Durr al-Mukhtār: Sharḥ Tanwīr al-Abṣār*. 8 vols. Cairo, 1386–89/1966–69. [Also Cairo: Muṣṭafā al-Bābī al-Ḥalabī 1966. Also *Ḥāshiyat al-'Allāmah al-Faqīh al-Fahhāmah al-Nabīh Khātimat al-Muḥaqqiqīn al-Shaykh Muḥammad Amīn al-Shahīr bi-Ibn 'Ābidīn, al-Musammā Radd al-Muḥtār*. Tab'ah 1. Quetta: Maktabah Mājidīyah, 1404/1984.]

________. ردّ المحتار على الدرّ المختار: شرح تنوير الأبصار. القاهرة، ١٣٨٦-٨٩/١٩٦٦-٦٩

________. *Al-'Uqūd al-Durrīyah fī Tanqīḥ al-Fatāwā al-Ḥāmidiyah* (latter by Ḥāmid ibn Muḥammad al-Qastamūnī al-Qunawī (d. 985/1577)). 2 vols. Būlāq, 1236, 1238, & 1300. [Also reprint Beirut: Dār al-Ma'rifah, 1974.]

________. العقود الدرّية فى تنقيح الفتاوى الحامدية. بولاق، ١٢٣٦

________. *Majmūāt Rasā'il Ibn 'Ābidīn*. Isṭānbūl: Sharikat Ṣaḥāyah 'Uthmānīyah Maṭbāḥsi, 1325/1907. [Also Beirut: Mu'assasat Fu'ād, 1978.]

________. مجموعة رسائل إبن عابدين. إستانبول: شركة صحاية عثمانية مطبحسى، ١٣٢٥/١٩٠٧

Maydānī, 'Abd al-Ghanī, al- (d. 1268/1851). *Al-Lubāb fī Sharḥ al-Kitāb*. 4 vols. Cairo, 1383/1963. [Also in the margin in al-'Abbādī (d. 800/1397). *Al-Jawharah al-Nayyirah li-Mukhtaṣar al-Qudūrī*. 2 vols. Cairo, 1322–1323.]

الميدانى، عبد الغنى (المتوفى ١٢٦٨/١٨٥١). اللباب فى شرح الكتاب. القاهرة، ١٣٨٣/١٩٦٣

Commission of Ottoman Jurists (1867-77). *Al-Majallah*. Constantinople, 1305. Also translated by C. A. Hooper. *The Civil Law of Palestine and Trans-Jordan*. 2 vols. Jerusalem, 1933. Also translated by Tyser, C. R. & Demetriades, D. G. & Haqqi, Ismail. *The Mejelle*. Lahore, 1967.

مجلّة الأحكام العدلية. قسطنطنية، ١٣٠٥

Ibn 'Ābidīn, 'Alā' al-Dīn (d. 1306/1888). *Qurrat 'Uyūn al-Akhyār Takmilat Radd al-Muḥtār 'alā al-Durr al-Mukhtār*. In vols. 7 & 8 in Ibn 'Ābidīn (d. 1252/1836). *Radd al-Muḥtār 'alā al-Durr al-Mukhtār*. 8 vols. Cairo, 1386–89/1966–69.

إبن عابدين، علاء الدين (المتوفى ١٣٠٦/١٨٨٨). قرّة عيون الأخيار تكملة ردّ المحتار على الدرّ المختار. مع ردّ المحتار على الدرّ المختار. القاهرة، ١٣٨٦-٨٩/١٩٦٦-٦٩

'Abd al-Ḥayy al-Lakhnawī, Abū al-Ḥasanāt Muḥammad (d. 1306/ 1888). *Sharḥ al-Wiqāyah ma'a Ḥāshiyat 'Umdat al-Ra'āyah*. Quetta, 1986.

عبد الحيّ اللكهنوى، أبو الحسنات محمد (المتوفى ١٣٠٦/١٨٨٨). شرح الوقاية مع حاشية عمدة الرعاية. كوءٹه، ١٩٨٦

Qadrī Pāshā al-Ḥanafī, Muḥammad (d. 1306/1888). *Al-Aḥkām al-Shar'īyah fī al-Aḥwāl al-Shakhsīyah.* Translated by Wasey Sterry & N. Abcarius. *Code of Mohammedan Personal Law According to the Hanafite School, by Mohammed Kadir Pasha.* London, 1914.

قدرى پاشا الحنفى، محمد (المتوفى ١٣٠٦/١٨٨٨). الأحكام الشرعية فى الأحوال الشخصية. لندن، ١٩١٤

'Abbāsī al-Ḥanafī al-Mahdī al-Miṣrī, Muḥammad, al- (d. 1315/1897). *al-Fatāwā al-Mahdīyah fī al-Waqā'i' al-Miṣrīyah.* 7 vols. Cairo, 1301–1304.

العبّاسى الحنفى المهدى المصرى، محمّد (المتوفى ١٣١٥/١٨٩٧). الفتاوى المهديّة فى الوقائع المصريّة. القاهرة، ١٣٠٤-١٣٠١

'Abd al-Ḥakīm al-Afghānī. *Kashf al-Ḥaqā'iq: Sharḥ Kanz al-Daqā'iq*. 2 vols. in 1. Cairo: al-Maktabah al-Adabīyah, 1318 & 1322. [Also Karachi: Idārat al-Qur'ān wa-al-'Ulūm al-Islāmīyah, 1987.

عبد الحكيم الأفغانى. كشف الحقائق: شرح كنز الدقائق. القاهرة: المكتبة الأدبية، ١٣١٨

'Alī Effendi. *Fatāwā 'Ali Effendi*. 2 vols. Constantinople, 1245.

على أفندى. فتاوى الأفندى. قسطنطنية، ١٢٤٥

Khaṭīb, Dawūd ibn Yūsuf. *Al-Fatāwa al-Ghiyāthīyah*. Al-Ṭab'ah 1. Bulaq: al-Maṭba'ah al-Amīrīyah, 1322. [Also Quetta: Maktabah Islāmīyah, 1403/1983.]

خطيب داوود بن يوسف. الفتاوى الغياثية. بولاق: المطبعة الأميرية، ١٣٢٢

Suwaysī, 'Abd al-Raḥmān, al-. *Talkhīṣ al-Nuṣūṣ al-Bahīyah min al-Fatāwā al-Mahdīyah*. Cairo, 1318.

السويسى، عبد الرحمان. تلخيص النصوص البهيّة من الفتاوى المهدية. القاهرة، ١٣١٨

Ṭarābulusī al-Ḥanafī, Muḥammad Kāmil ibn Muṣṭafā ibn Maḥmūd, al-. *Al-Fatāwā al-Kāmilīyah fī al-Ḥawādith al-Ṭarābulusīyah*. Cairo, 1313/1895.

الطرابلسى الحنفى، محمد كامل بن مصطفى بن محمود. الفتاوى الكاملية فى الحوادث الطرابلسية. القاهرة، ١٣١٣/١٨٩٥

Ṭūrī, Muḥammad ibn Ḥusayn ibn 'Alī, al-. *Takmilat al-Baḥr al-Rā'iq: Sharḥ Kanz al-Daqā'iq*. In vol. 8 in Ibn Nujaym (d. 970/1563). *Al-Baḥr al-Rā'iq*. 8 vols. Cairo, 1333.

الطورى، محمد بن حسين بن على. تكملة البحر الرائق: شرح كنز الدقائق. مع البحر الرائق. القاهرة، ١٣٣٣

INDEX

'Abbādī al-Ḥaddād , Abū Bakr ibn 'Alī, 130
'Abbāsī al-Ḥanafī al-Mahdī al-Miṣrī, Muḥammad, 139
'Abd al-Ḥakīm al-Afghānī, 139
'Abd al-Ḥalīm al-Lakhnawī, Aḥmad 'Abd al-Ḥalīm ibn Mawlānā Amīn Allāh, 120
'Abd al-Ḥayy al-Lakhnawī, Abū al-Ḥasanāt Muḥammad, 139
Abdur Rahim, Sir, 25
Abū Ḥanīfah, 27
Abū Ḥanīfah, al-Nu'mān ibn Thābit ibn Zūṭā, 115
Abū Ḥanīfah, al-Nu'mān ibn Muḥammad (d. 363/974), 125
Abū Yūsuf, 29
Abū Yūsuf Ya'qūb ibn Ibrāhīm ibn Ḥabīb al-Kūfī al-Anṣārī, 123
Akhsīkathī, Muḥammad ibn Muḥammad, 137
'Alī Effendi, 139
Amīr Bādshāh, Muḥammad Amīn, 119
Anqirāwī, Muḥammad ibn Ḥusayn, 136
As'ad Shaykh al-lslām ibn Abū Bakr al-Qaysarānī al-lskandarānī, 134

aṣl
and *qawā'id uṣūliyyah*, 18
Awrangzeb 'Ālamgīr, Sulṭān Muḥiy al-Dīn, 136
'Aynī 'Antabī al-Ḥanafī, Abū Muḥammad Maḥmūd ibn Aḥmad ibn Mūsā ibn Aḥmad ibn Ḥusayn ibn Ysusf Badr al-Dīn, 131
'Azmī'zādah, Musṭafā ibn Muḥammad, 119

Bābartī, Akmal al-Dīn Muḥammad ibn Maḥmūd, 130
Bahr al-'Ulūm, Muḥammad 'Abd al-'Alī ibn Niẓām al-Dīn Muḥammad al-Anṣārī al-Lakhnawī, 120
Bazdawī Fakhr al-Islam, 'Alī ibn Muḥammad ibn al-Ḥusayn, 116
Bazzāzī al-Kurdurī, Ḥafīẓ al-Dīn Muḥammad ibn Muḥammad, 131
Bidāyat al-Mubtadi' al-Qudūrī, 38
Bihārī, Muḥibb Allāh ibn 'Abd al-Shukūr, 119
Bukhārī, 'Abd al-'Azīz, 117

case method, 38
and *fiqh*, 39

Dabūsī, Abū Zayd 'Ubayd Allāh ibn 'Umar 'Īsā, 116, 126

faqīh
methodology of, 23
fuqahā'
grades of, 29

gate of *ijtihād*, 23
Al-Ghazālī, 24, 26

Ḥalabī, Burhān al-Dīn Ibrāhīm ibn Muḥammad ibn Ibrāhīm, 133
Ḥalabī, Zayn al-Dīn Abū 'Azzī Ṭāhir ibn al-Ḥasan ibn Ḥabīb, 117
Ḥāmid ibn Muṣṭafā Effendī Qāḍī al-'Askar al-'Uthmānīyah, 119
Ḥanafī school, 42
Ḥaṣkafī, 'Alā' al-Dīn ibn Aḥmad ibn Muḥammad, 119, 135

Ibn 'Ābidīn, 'Alā' al-Dīn, 138
Ibn 'Ābidīn, Muḥammad Amīn ibn 'Umar ibn 'Abd al-'Azīz, 120
Ibn 'Ābidīn, Muḥammad Amīn ibn 'Uthmān ibn 'Abd al-'Azīz, 137
Ibn 'Alā', 'Ālim, 130
Ibn al-Ḥalabī, Riyaḍ al-Dīn Muḥammad ibn Ibrāhīm, 118
Ibn Ḥamzah, 'Abd al-Ḥalīm ibn Pīr Qadam, 134
Ibn al-Humām al-Siwasī al-Iskandarī, Kamāl al-Dīn Muḥammad ibn Humām al-Dīn 'Abd al-Wāḥid ibn 'Abd al-Ḥamīd, 118, 132
Ibn al-Malak, 'Izz al-Dīn 'Abd al-Laṭīf ibn 'Abd al-'Azīz ibn Amīn Firishtah, 117
Ibn Nujaym, Zayn al-'Ābidīn ibn Ibrāhīm, 118, 133
Ibn Qāḍī Samāwah, Badr al-Dīn Maḥmūd ibn Isrā'īl, 131
ijtihād
as a source, 32
closing the gate of, 23
Izmīrī, Sulaymān ibn 'Abd Allāh, 119

Jamālī, 'Alā' al-Dīn 'Alī ibn Aḥmad, 132
Jaṣṣāṣ al-Rāzī, Abū Bakr Aḥmad ibn 'Alī, 115, 126
jurists
grades of, 29

Karkhī, 'Abd Allāh ibn al-Ḥusayn, 115
Kāsānī, Abū Bakr ibn Mas'ūd, 127
Kawākibī, Muḥammad ibn al-Ḥasan, 119, 136
Khādimī, Abū Sa'īd Muḥammad ibn Muṣṭafā ibn 'Uthmān, 137
Khaṣṣāf, Abū Bakr Aḥmad ibn 'Umar al-Shaybānī, 124
Khaṭīb, Dawūd ibn Yūsuf, 139
Khayr al-Dīn ibn Aḥmad ibn Nūr al-Dīn 'Alī ibn Zayn al-Dīn ibn 'Abd al-Wahhāb al-Ayyūbī al-'Ulaymī al-Fārūqī al-Ramlī, 135
Kūhistānī, Shams al-Dīn Muḥammad, 132

Maḥallawī al-Ḥanafī, Muḥammad ibn 'Abd al-Raḥmān, 121
Mālik ibn Anas, 26
Marghinānī al-Rushdānī Burhān al-Dīn, 'Alī ibn Abū Bakr ibn 'Abd al-Jalīl al-Farghānī, 128
Māturīdī, Muḥammad ibn Muḥammad, 115
Mawṣilī al-Buldajī, Abū al-Faḍl Majd al-Dīn 'Abd Al-lāh ibn Maḥmūd ibn Mawdūd, 129
Maydānī, 'Abd al-Ghanī, 138
Muḥammad al-Shaybāni, 29, 32
mukhtaṣars, 34
  and *Bidāyat al-Mubtadi'*, 38
Mullā Jīwan, Aḥmad ibn Abī Sa'īd [Shaykh Mullā], 120
Mullā Khusraw, Muḥammad ibn Farāmurz ibn 'Alī, 118, 132
Mullā Miskīn al-Harawī, Mu'īn al-Dīn Muḥammad ibn Ibrāhīm al-Farāhī, 131
mutūn mu'tabarah, 36

Nābulusī, 'Abd al-Ghanī ibn Ismā'īl, 120
Nasafī al-Māturīdī, Najm al-Dīn Abū Ḥafṣ 'Umar ibn Muḥammad ibn Aḥmad, 115, 127
Nasafī, Ḥafīẓ al-Dīn Abū al-Barakāt 'Abd Allāh ibn Aḥmad ibn Maḥmūd, 117, 129

Qāḍī Khān, Fakhr al-Dīn al-Ḥasan ibn Manṣūr al-Uzjānī al-Farghānī, 128
Qādiri Effendi, 'Abd al-Qādir ibn Yṡuf Naqīb'zādah al-Ḥanafī al-Ḥalabī, 136
Qaḍī'zādah, Shams al-Dīn, 133
Qadrī Pāshā al-Ḥanafī, Muḥammad, 139
Qārī al-Harawī, Ālī ibn Sulṭān Muḥammad, 134
qualified *mujtahid*, 87
Qudūrī al-Baghdādī, Abū al-Ḥusayn Aḥmad ibn Muḥammad, 126

Ruḥawī, Abū Zakariyā' Yaḥyā, 121

Sa'd Allāh 'Īsā Sa'dī Shalabī, 132
Ṣadr al-Sharī'ah al-Thānī al-Maḥbūbī, 'Ubayd Al-lāh ibn Mas'ūd, 117, 130
Ṣadr al-Sharī'ah, 18
Ṣafī al-Hindī, Muḥammad ibn 'Abd al-Raḥīm, 120
Sajawandī, Sirāj al-Dīn Abū Ṭāhir Muḥammad ibn Muḥammad ibn 'Abd al-Rashīd, 128
Samarqandī, Abū al-Layth Naṣr ibn Muḥammad ibn Aḥmad ibn Ibrāhīm, 126
Samarqandī, Abū Bakr 'Alā' al-Dīn al-Mansūr Muḥammad ibn Aḥmad, 116, 127
Al-Sarakhsī, 33

Sarakhsī, Shams al-A'immah Abū Bakr Muḥammad ibn Abī Sahl Aḥmad, 116, 126
schools of law, 41
  Ḥanafī school, 42
Al-Shāfi'ī, 33
Shāshī al-Samarqandī, Abū Ya'qūb Isḥāq ibn Ibrāhīm, 115
Shaybānī, Muḥammad ibn al-Ḥasan, 123
Shaykh'zādāh, 'Abd al-Raḥmān ibn Muḥammad ibn Sulaymān, 135
Shiblī, Shihāb al-Dīn Aḥmad, 132
Shurunbulālī al-Ḥanafī, Abū al-lkhlāṣ Ḥasan ibn Ammār al-Wafā'ī, 134
Shurunbulālī, Muḥammad ibn Su'ūd, 137
Suwaysī, 'Abd al-Raḥmān, 140

Ṭaḥāwī, Aḥmad ibn Muḥammad, 137
Ṭaḥāwī, Abū Ja'far Aḥmad ibn Muḥammad ibn Salāmah al-Ḥajrī, 125
Ṭā'ī, Musṭafā ibn Muḥammad, 137
takhrīj, 23
  meaning of, 29
  process of, 41
Tamīmī al-Dārī, Taqī al-Dīn ibn 'Abd al-Qādir, 134
taqlīd
  and Pakistan law, 27
  in Islamic law, 27
  literal meaning, 24
  meaning of, 23
  technical meaning, 24
Ṭarābulusī 'Alā' al-Dīn Kawsaj Abū al-Ḥasan al-Ḥanafī, 'Alī ibn Khalīl, 131
Ṭarābulusī al-Ḥanafī, Muḥammad Kāmil ibn Muṣṭafā ibn Maḥmūd, 140
Tarāsūsī al-Ḥanafī, Najm al-Dīn Abū Isḥāq Ibrāhīm ibn 'Imād al-Dīn Abū al-Ḥasan 'Alī ibn Aḥmad ibn 'Abd al-Ṣamad, 130
theory of adjudication, 23
Timurtāshi al-Ghazzī al-Ḥanafī, Shams al-Dīn, 134
Ṭūrī, Muḥammad ibn Ḥusayn ibn 'Alī, 140

Ustarūshanī, Muḥammad ibn Maḥmūd, 129
uṣūl al-fiqh
  formation of principles, 18

Zayla'ī, Fakhr al-Dīn 'Uthmān ibn 'Alī ibn Mihjān al-Barī'ī, 129

About This Book

This is the only text that provides a scientific and methodological reason for following a single school. Most texts, when they are justifying Taqlid, make emotional appeals and point to the piety of the earlier jurists and the founders of schools. The present work explains why it is a necessity to follow a single school. It also points out and explains why "picking and choosing" opinions, randomly from different schools, is wrong. The text also elaborates upon the rules for issuing fatwas and outlines the methodology for issuing rulings in the present times. The existing "one-liners," the text shows, are difficult to accept. The text focuses on a single school, but what is said is easily applied to other schools.

www.ingramcontent.com/pod-product-compliance
Lightning Source LLC
Chambersburg PA
CBHW071439180526
45170CB00001B/388
* 9 7 8 1 5 4 1 2 8 4 9 9 9 *